I Thought You'd Be Faster

The Quest to Become an Athlete

To Ann —
You're an
inspiration!

Amy Moritz

ISBN: 978-0-692-96888-8 (print)

"We must make the choices that enable us to fulfill the deepest capacities of our real selves."
—Thomas Merton

To my family. Thank you for allowing me to make the difficult, at times illogical, choices.

Table of Contents

Chapter 1: Skulking On the Edges

The Call of the Athlete

This was a stupid way to die—clinging to the hand of a twenty-year-old named Ashley in the middle of Keuka Lake.

OK, I wasn't exactly in the middle of the lake. I was probably about fifty meters off shore, encased in my new neoprene wetsuit with my hands and feet numb from the sixty-degree water temperature. Ashley, a trained life guard, was laying on her surfboard, trying to get me to stop crying.

For the record: I wasn't full-on crying. I was trying desperately *not* to cry, which if you've ever tried to stop yourself from a full-on cry you know can actually be worse than the crying itself. My breaths were shallow and rapid. Tears trickled into my goggles. Swimming was difficult enough on its own without adding my own brand of limiting behaviors, including erratic breathing and foggy goggle lenses.

I was failing, and I knew it.

It was my first triathlon, held in June 2008 in Keuka, a small town in central New York State. The event was on the lake of the same name and staged on the campus of Keuka College. The region is part of the Finger Lakes, known for wineries and fishing and relaxing weekend getaways. But there was nothing relaxing about my visit. I had been in full-on panic mode for days. Swimming was my weakest point. When I decided to train for a triathlon the first step had been to learn how to swim. I made it a lighthearted piece of my story. I'd wave my hand casually and call learning to swim "just a detail." But the detail scared the crap out of me. I was learning to swim at the age of thirty-five so that I could complete a triathlon. If I stopped to think about it, just for a minute, it sounded like the most ridiculous idea in the world.

Learning to swim as an adult has an entirely different set of challenges than learning as a child. First of all, you know the risks. You've seen enough episodes of *Law & Order* to envision your body floating up among some fishermen days after you went in for a "quick summer swim." Secondly, you've had more time to become self-conscious—particularly if you're a woman and have read decades' worth of magazine stories on finding the right swimsuit for your body type. Finally, there's the mounting pressure of being goal-oriented. I was learning to swim not only to churn out laps in the pool but as a means to an end. I wanted to be an athlete. I wanted to do a triathlon. I needed to develop this skill set, and quickly. Patience was never one of my virtues, and this became all the more apparent—not to mention *frustrating*—while learning to swim. There were so many things to think about—where my arm was, how my hand was positioned, how much I was turning my body, if I was turning my body too much, how I was kicking, how I was turning my head to breathe, how often I was breathing . . .

My stroke was choppy. I couldn't swim in a straight line. I could not perform alternate breathing no matter how hard I tried. I had serious doubts I would ever get to dry land and onto my bike during this triathlon.

While this triathlon world was new to me, sports had always been part of my life. I grew up in a family of diehard Buffalo sports fans. We watched professional football (the Bills), hockey (the Sabres), and minor-league baseball (the Bisons). We followed local college basketball. We read the sports pages and always had a game, any game, on the television over the weekend. I came from a family of proud and loyal fans. Of course, no one in my family seemed to ever *play* sports. I had no immediate role models when it came to participation.

I was glued to the TV set the summer of 1984. I was eleven years old and was mesmerized by the Los Angeles Olympics, particularly by gymnast

Mary Lou Retton. I idolized Mary Lou. She became the first American woman to win an Olympic gold medal in gymnastics, winning the All-Around title with a dramatic final vault and a perfect score of 10 to take the title. I cut out every article I could find on her (recall this was pre-Internet days) and bought box after box of Wheaties which featured her in a triumphant pose, arms raised above her head in her red, white, and blue Team USA leotard. I even got my hair to look like hers, chopping it from below my shoulders to a layered, tightly cropped style that barely went below my ears.

That was as close as I'd get to being an athlete—copying Mary Lou Retton's hairstyle.

I turned my love of sports into a career as a sports reporter, covering everything from high school to college to the pros.

I moved in the athletic world, but I was not *of* the athletic world. This was great for a long time. For nearly two decades. It was fine . . . until it wasn't enough.

Part of me still wanted to be an athlete.

A secret part of me.

I didn't dare say it too loudly because people would laugh, people would most surely laugh. I was the girl who injured herself playing miniature golf. I was the girl who described herself with a perpetual weight problem and physical inadequacies. I wasn't coordinated. I wasn't on a team. I wasn't going to win anything. Competition of any kind made me so nervous I wanted to roll up into a ball, plug my ears, and forget the whole damn thing.

I was *not* an athlete.

And yet . . .

And *yet* there was something inside of me that whispered I was.

Ridiculous, right?

I'm not an athlete. I mean, I exercise to stay healthy and lose weight. But I'm not an athlete, even as I write this book.

And yet . . .

By the time I started to pay attention to this whisper I was in my thirties. Far too late to become an athlete, right? Don't you need skill to be an athlete? Isn't it too late for me?

And yet . . .

The Last Swimmer

Here I was. In an ice-cold Keuka Lake on a hot June morning trying desperately to maneuver my way around a 750-meter swim course.

I considered asking for a water rescue. I knew the rules said if that happened I couldn't finish the race, but maybe they'd let me continue on unofficially. Perhaps this whole idea of a triathlon was too much for me to take on.

Ten backstrokes, then a rest; ten backstrokes, then a rest. The doubts flooded my brain all the while my body continued to float along the course ten backstrokes at a time. Failing? Maybe I was. Technically I wasn't "swimming." I was floating and creating my own stroke—the jogging breaststroke. But was I really failing?

When I put my foot on the beach, one of the volunteers shouted so loud it echoes in my head to this day: *"THE LAST SWIMMER IS OUT OF THE WATER!"*

I was the last swimmer. Dead last. I looked behind and every single water craft that had been used to ensure the safety of the swimmers was lined up behind—surfboards, kayaks, canoes, small watercraft. The race had started packing up the beach area by the time I had made my way around the giant buoys. I had no trouble finding my bike in the transition area because it was the only bike left. Everyone else was already out, cycling away, on the second leg of the swim-bike-run course.

But I had finished the swim.

I finished the swim!

I *finished* the *SWIM!*

My brain was flooded with positivity. I came out of the water under my own power. I had faced the scariest thing in my life—the crippling hold of doubt while playing a mental game of "worst-case scenario" in the open water—and made it through. Was it pretty? Most certainly not. And it definitely wasn't fast. But I raced up to the transition area, where I would change from swim to bike and from bike to run. I wiggled out of my wetsuit and onto my bike and headed out for the rest of the race, filled with a sense of accomplishment and something else . . .

Was this fearlessness?

Somewhere inside of me there was an athlete yearning to get out. She didn't need to be the best. She only wanted the freedom to play—to move and be challenged and have fun and laugh. She wanted to push herself. She wanted to fail. She wanted to learn lessons and scrape her knee and cross the finish line in triumph.

The athlete inside of me was tired of watching everyone else have the fun. And she was tired of watching me stumble through life on the sidelines. She was no longer whispering, no longer timid. She was out in full force. And she had quite a journey to take me on.

Catching Foul Balls

Grandma's porch. It was the most glorious place in the summer.

My grandparents, Eleanore and Sylvester, lived in a first-ring suburb of Buffalo on a corner lot. The one-story brick house had a porch that stretched along the side of the house. It gave a perfect view of the neighborhood, so Gram could keep an eye on the comings and goings of everyone as she sat in her chair. She was a large woman with a larger-than-life presence; her white hair with tinges of gray fell in short waves around her face. Gram had a permanent spot on the porch—to the right of the side door which opened to the dining room. That was Gram's seat. Gramps had his own seat—on the other side of the door. He would sit there in the summer, wearing a short-sleeved button-down shirt coupled with shorts and knee socks. His hair kept its dark brown color and was slicked back off his face. He balanced my grandmother's boisterousness with a quiet, thoughtful demeanor, though he was always quick with a quip and a failure to suppress the smirk that would creep across his face.

Gramps sat in a folding rocking chair that angled from the corner, with a tray table to his right.

That's where the radio sat.

It was a portable transistor radio. Its brown leather cover was frayed in a dozen different places from constant use and braving the elements. It had dials and tunings and flips and switches and it amazed me that my grandparents could easily find what they were looking for with a gentle nudge of a nob. It often was set to a music station, playing polkas which all sounded the same to me but were full of life and smiles and the possibility of dancing around in circles until you were dizzy and fell down. (This is how ten-year-olds polka, of course.) When it wasn't polka time, it was softly playing standards from the 1940s—Perry Como and Bing Crosby and the Andrews Sisters.

But Sunday afternoons the radio was always tuned to baseball.

The games were those of the Buffalo Bisons, a minor league team with deep roots in the city and deep roots in my family. The team had been around, in some form, since 1877. My grandparents had been watching and rooting for the Bisons their entire lifetimes. And when I visited on those Sunday afternoons, between rounds on the Slip-N-Slide and swinging on the hammock, I joined my grandparents on the porch with a glass of lemonade and caught snippets of the game.

My grandfather had a scorecard in his lap, tracking the plays as he listened to Pete Weber, the radio voice of the Buffalo Bisons, describe the game. I went over to watch and he showed me what he was doing. When a player got a hit, he'd draw a line to cover a corner of the square. When a player scored, he colored a dot in the center of what was now a diamond. If a player struck out while swinging, his box was filled with a *K*; if it was a called third-strike, it was a backwards *K*. But he told me not to worry about that right now. So it went as players moved around the bases.

Gramps loved stats. He kept them for pretty much everything and for no apparent reason other than he loved to keep track of things. He loved the numbers.

I didn't particularly love numbers, but I loved baseball. I loved all sports. Which is why I was so bummed out in third grade when a student-teacher took my classmate Eric aside. During free time I would see them together, pouring over a newspaper at the teacher's desk. They did math problems based on the baseball standings. The student-teacher, a young man, showed Eric how to figure out baseball standings and other statistics. Eric was "advanced" at math. I was not; I was good at reading and writing—at least that was what I was told. Still, I wished I was able to learn how to figure out the baseball standings like the guys were doing at the teacher's desk.

Maybe I wasn't good at math and I wasn't supposed to understand the stats.

I didn't say anything. I was in third grade. You don't question your teachers in third grade.

Maybe baseball stats weren't for me.

But *baseball* was.

I knew this because of my grandmother.

Gram loved to tell stories. The same ones over and over again, until I believed I had once watched baseball games at Buffalo's old Offermann Stadium, even though the structure was demolished eleven years before I was born.

Gram's family didn't have a lot of money in the Depression Era of the 1930s. Her father liked to cash his paycheck at the neighborhood bar and drink away his income, leaving his family short on rent. They constantly moved from rental to rental within a three-block radius. At times her stories offered glimpses at the darkness in her past. They were brief, nearly throwaway vignettes.

There was the time her father chased her around outside the house with a broken ketchup bottle. "I was the black sheep," she liked to say, noting that in her day "there was no such thing as child abuse." There was the time she and her sister Doris went out for a fish fry and laughed and danced and ended up with not enough money to pay the bill. They did dishes and all was forgiven, but the embarrassment certainly lingered. She struggled to read Polish, which was a problem as a member of a proud Polish-Catholic family. She misspoke at her confirmation, wanting to take the name "Angeline," which she thought was so beautiful and elegant, but ending up with "Agnes" instead. The darkness at times was tinged with regret. She never graduated from high school. She left a month early. Her family needed her to get a job so they could afford to send her older sister to nursing school. For this sacrifice she harshly criticized herself with the label "dunce."

These stories were hard to hear.

But then she'd talk about baseball and everything would change. A smile crept over her entire face, bringing warmth to her skin and happiness to her eyes. Oh, they were poor, all right, but they did have ingenuity. And that's how they found their way into baseball games.

In the summer, she and her brothers would head over to Offermann Stadium, searching for baseballs hit outside the stadium walls during batting practice. Sometimes her brothers muscled for the balls hit outside the cozy confines of the small stadium, collecting enough for all the siblings. They would turn in the baseballs to the usher at the gate. One returned baseball got you into the game for free.

(Hey—those baseballs cost money, and the baseball team wasn't flush with cash itself.)

Sometimes, Gram would say, the usher would slip them a nickel to buy themselves a treat at the concession stand.

Baseball played a role in my grandparents' courtship, too. They would go to games in the years before World War II, taking the street car to the stadium then walking home, saving the fare to spend on ice cream sundaes—Mexican sundaes for Gram, butterscotch sundaes for Gramps.

It seemed sports played a central role in my grandmother's life. And so sports became the soundtrack of my childhood. We watched the Buffalo Bills football in the fall, with family Sunday dinners planned for halftime so as not to miss too much of the action. We listened to Buffalo Bisons baseball in the summer and went to a handful of games at the cavernous and deteriorating War Memorial Stadium.

We went to college basketball games, entertained by stories of the glories of decades past, when weekend doubleheaders drew thousands of fans; back before Buffalo became a pro-sports town that looked past its small, mid-major college teams and let them fade to the edge of relevancy.

We planned Christmas vacation to include the Buffalo Sabres' open practice, when the hockey team would entertain fans at "the Aud" in downtown Buffalo with skills and drills and a scrimmage peppered with pranks. Afterward, my brother and I would race around the tunnels to find our favorite players stationed around the arena to sign autographs.

Through it all, my grandmother and my mother were the biggest sports fans I knew. They told stories about what they watched growing up: baseball was my grandmother's passion, while my mother loved college basketball and football. It never occurred to me it was unusual for women to be knowledgeable about sports. I grew up in their world of intense sports fandom, and it was a world I embraced and loved.

I was captivated by the stories of the teams and players and how they seemed to flow alongside my family history. It drew me on a deeper level, one that wanted to participate, to be in the game, not just in the stands. But this was the 1980s, and my opportunities to connect to the athletic world as a pre-teen girl were few and far between. This lack delayed my development.

But it never destroyed my desire.

Cut from the Team

There had to be fifty girls in the gym, or at least it felt like fifty girls. There were so many, most of whom I didn't know and all of whom were taller than me, and all of them seemed to know what they were doing.

It was the second day of tryouts for the junior varsity basketball team, and I was lost.

I had never played basketball aside from shooting baskets in our driveway. I'm not sure how tall the rim was that perched awkwardly on the side of our narrow driveway, but I doubt it was regulation height. Even if it was, it was difficult to get off a good shot, since the hoop was alongside the driveway instead of at the end. That meant the farthest back you could go was about three feet—not very helpful for practicing anything more than offensive rebound put-backs. And I was far too short to earn a spot as a forward.

Still, I signed up for tryouts and showed up for practice. It was the first time I ever ran suicides—the conditioning drill where players stand at the baseline then run to the free throw line and back, the half court line and back, the far free throw line and back, and finally the far baseline and back. We were supposed to complete that in thirty-five seconds.

I was always last.

By a lot.

Was I intimidated? Hell, yes. All these girls had played before. All of them had gone to basketball camp. It quickly occurred to me that junior varsity wasn't where you learned to play basketball (just as triathlons aren't where you learn to swim). It was where you went when you had achieved a certain level of competence on the court.

At the end of the second practice, the coach called me over.

I was cut.

I was disappointed, of course, but not surprised.

Still, the coach encouraged me. "I watched you," she said. "You ran through the line every time on those sprints, even though you were last. We just have a lot of girls back who played last year. You should practice the drills we did and try out next year."

Next year seemed so far away for a teenage girl. Three hundred sixty-five days! And how was I going to get better? My parents didn't play sports. I heard my mom once talk about playing basketball when she was in elementary school. They played six-on-six—and only one girl could cross half-court.

That wasn't going to help me much.

Plus . . . I wanted to be part of the team *now*. I wanted to belong to something in the sports world. I wanted to learn things firsthand, things that I couldn't discover just by watching on television. I needed to find a new option.

Then, in a flash of brilliance, I remembered one of my family sports stories—Gramps was a statistician for the Canisius College men's basketball team. The man who loved math found himself as part of the official scorer's table during those famed Little Three Doubleheaders featuring the Western New York college teams from Canisius, Niagara, and St. Bonaventure. He got the gig because his brother was the team doctor. He still had all the score sheets from the 1970s, mimeographed copies of point totals and rebounds and steals.

So what if in third grade I wasn't good enough for the special math lessons from the sports pages? I could learn to keep stats for basketball just like I learned to keep a baseball scorecard.

The girls' varsity basketball coach was an English teacher at my junior high. I wrote him a letter asking if I could be a statistician for the team. He found me and invited me to practice.

The next five years I never missed a practice or a game, trading in my playing aspirations for a spot on the team as a manager. I kept stats. I helped out at practice gathering equipment, running the scoreboard during drills, and filling water bottles. I would rebound for players as they took extra shots before or after practice. On rare occasions I would step into a drill to fill in for a missing player. Mostly I watched and listened and learned the basics of offense (square your shoulders to the basket, follow your shot, curl around the screen) and defense (communicating with your teammates was the most important aspect here).

It was surprisingly easy to go from the desire to play basketball to being part of the support staff instead. I had no history with being a basketball player—no prior teams or camp experiences. My only hands-on background with basketball came through gym class and occasional shooting games in the driveway.

My desire to be *part* of the team exceeded my desire to *play* for the team. To become good enough to put on a uniform—even to sit on the bench—would take me too long, and time was not on my side. By the time I had decided I wanted to play basketball, everyone else had already been to camps and played on summer league teams. I was starting a few years behind from square one. Plus, it was a road I knew nothing about. I didn't even know where to start if I wanted to learn the fundamentals of playing basketball. But I did know how to fill water balls, retrieve missed shots in a shoot-around, and keep track of points, assists, and rebounds. It wasn't on the court, but it was an important part of keeping the team running.

This is where I could make my niche in the sports world.

My niche grew quickly as the varsity coach/English teacher tasked me with writing the game recaps for the local paper and calling the television stations with our score. He thought it was a great opportunity for me. "You love sports and you love to write. You should think about being a sportswriter." The statement was an epiphany for me, and I don't mean in the casual sense that people use the word "epiphany" to describe a moment of insight. I mean a deeply felt epiphany, one where angels sang and the sky brightened and my whole heart opened up to say "YES! THAT'S IT!"

I could be a sportswriter.

This is how I can be part of the athletic world.

This is my calling.

My energy went into this pursuit of becoming a sportswriter. I chose St. Bonaventure in Olean, NY, for its reputation as a solid journalism school and because I would be able to continue my behind-the-scenes role as a manager for the women's basketball team. I hustled for internships and freelance writing gigs, and I quickly learned it never hurts to ask if someone might need an article on a game you're already going to be attending.

It took two years after graduation for me to land my first full-time sports reporting gig at the small *Olean Times-Herald* covering my alma mater. It took two years of hustle to get an interview, and then a job, at *The Buffalo News*.

I had achieved my goal! I was writing for a major newspaper about sports.

And yet it didn't quite seem like enough on a personal level.

I had met interesting people, watched a ton of games, interviewed players and coaches, and learned some of the ins and outs of being an elite athlete. But something was still missing. I moved *around* the sports world; I worked on its edges; I was *shadowing* what I really wanted to be.

What I really wanted to be was an athlete.

I thought that opportunity had died with my two-day stint in junior varsity basketball. And who the hell was I to be an athlete? Athletes came from athletic families. Maybe their parents played a different sport, but they understood the athletic game. I didn't come from a family of athletes. I came from a family of sports fan.

Then Gram died.

And I knew it was no longer time to be content skulking on the edges of being an athlete.

Losing Grandma, Finding Myself

My grandmother was a stubborn, old, Polish woman.

That's how I began the eulogy I gave at her funeral. For all the stories Gram told of what were her golden years—particularly those old baseball games and her courtship with my grandfather—she was to me an old Polish woman. The stories of late-night card playing and going to the Printer's Mass at 1 a.m. were not just from a bygone era, but a bygone version of my grandmother.

In my lifetime, her activity sharply decreased. When I was a child, she orchestrated her cherished Sunday family dinners—lavish affairs with linen table cloths, good china, and an overwhelming number of options. By the time I was in high school, the tradition devolved to pizza and wings—something which made the kids happy, in part because the Sunday family tradition took on the unhappy heaviness of obligation. But it never quite sat well with Gram, who saw some of the things she loved most decline in importance.

Then her health declined.

My father and I would talk about "the Gram situation" on our hikes. I would lament that she needed to see a doctor. He agreed, but knew his mother-in-law too well. She would not go to a doctor. She was hospitalized a grand total of once in her youth, when she contracted trichinosis from her habit of tasting raw meat to make sure it was fresh. Then again in her sixties when she was diagnosed with uterine cancer. She survived the surgery and the radiation treatment. That was her second time in the hospital. Third time, she said, and she wouldn't come back.

As her health started to get worse, she refused to see anyone about it. Stubborn. That was the most popular way to describe my grandmother, usually offered in deflated tones by people she had bested or outlasted. It was invoked negatively with a hope that she would change her ways, change her views, change her behavior. If only she would stop living in the past or living in fear, they would say.

Her stubbornness was not hers alone. It was a family trait, one I could see in my mother and one I certainly saw in myself—still do, in fact. As time went on, I came to see how that stubbornness could be a strength, how I could harness it for good—to motivate myself when doubt crept into my brain, for instance, or to make difficult decisions about relationships. Within that stubbornness is often the will of my heart, which no one completely understands but me. Her stubbornness was a gift to me, even as it pained me to watch Gram's stubbornness result in a complete shutdown.

Her health got worse. She stopped going to daily Mass, part of her bargain with God for getting her through the cancer. That was the first clue something was wrong, but since she refused help, everyone let it slide as her health continued to slide. By the time she reached seventy-five, Gram was under a self-induced house arrest. Her world shrank to her bedroom, the couch, and the bathroom.

She would not see a doctor.

Not until it was too late.

After two years of being alive but no longer living, Gram finally went to the hospital after she became unresponsive from high blood sugar. In the course of six months she went from the hospital to a nursing home to the hospital and finally a hospice facility, where she would spend the final two weeks of her life.

What killed her exactly is a mystery. She was diagnosed with Parkinson's disease. ("You and the Pope," my dad told her, referencing Pope John Paul II. I found it amusing. She did not.) She had all kinds of issues with her lower intestines and bladder. She wasn't officially diagnosed as a Type 2 diabetic, but her sugar and insulin levels were problematic. Her previously overweight body had atrophied from a combination of lack of use and poor nutrition. She was a physical mess and had been for years.

While she died on April 18, 2001, she stopped living long before then.

It broke my heart to watch her give up over those final years. In the months after the funeral, as I tried to regain my emotional center, I decided I didn't want to go down like that.

Gram's life story was full of vibrancy, but her slow decline into a sad ending overshadowed it all. I wanted a vibrant life story. And I heard my inner athlete calling to me. If I wanted to live big, my athletic voice said, I needed to take care of myself. My health was fine for a young woman approaching thirty, but my lifestyle could be better. If I wanted to live big, I needed practices to support those dreams. I needed daily routines to put me in the best possible position to be active and creative and take on new challenges. That meant learning about nutrition and fitness and feeding my soul. Inch by inch, I started to change my habits. I started to toss the junk-food diet—so easy to fall into with a sportswriter's schedule and the ubiquitous offerings of pizza—and began to eat a more vegetarian-based diet.

Changing my lifestyle became the outlet for my stubbornness and for my grief over losing Gram. It wasn't nearly as difficult to give up things like chicken wings and pepperoni pizza as some of my friends imagined. There were bigger gains to be had by skipping lunch via vending machine. I wanted a big life more than I wanted a quick and easy hamburger. Spending post-deadline Saturday nights at the bar with co-workers was fun in the moment, but left me feeling sluggish and tired the next day, and with increasing frequency the day after that. I pulled back from those outings because there were other things I wanted to do.

My inner athlete was calling. I started taking introductory yoga classes and power walking. I kept quiet about most of it. I mean, "power walking" is something retirees do in Floridian malls, right? But slowly I started seeing changes in my energy level. I started seeing changes in my body. I started to want more for myself. I started to have the confidence to take risks.

It was time for me to take a leap of faith.

That's how I ended up sitting in tears at the top of a thirty-foot pole in Colorado.

Chapter 2: You're Nuts!

Taking a Leap of Faith

This was a stupid way to die.

The first time I truly had that thought was in Winter Park, Colorado. It was a September day with mild temperatures and the clearest of blue skies. I had climbed thirty feet up a telephone pole, strapped into a harness with a helmet slightly askew on my head. I was supposed to stand up on this tiny platform—barely big enough to hold my butt—jump off, and try to grab a trapeze bar ten feet away.

How exactly did I end up here?

In the years after my grandmother's death the call to be an athlete grew stronger. I still eschewed the notion I could be an athlete, but I wanted to do something . . . *adventurous*. My circle of friends was broke (or always claimed to be) and non-committal. They were the type of friends who get all excited with you over coffee, talk up the adventure, add details to the dream, then abruptly back out when plans are presented. It was frustrating and limiting. And the solution, it turned out, was easily in my control.

I longed to go cycling on a long trip or try backpacking for a few days. I'd wistfully read outdoor magazines and cut out articles with destinations for hiking which seemed close and affordable. I'd devour yoga magazines looking for retreat options. I looked for anything that would take me out of Western New York, not because of disdain but rather because I needed to challenge my comfort zone. My friends loved to dream with me, but never wanted to take action. It was never a good time, it was never a good financial situation . . . it just was never going to be good for them.

But for me, it was time to stop dreaming about climbing mountains and exploring trails. It was time to stop putting preconceived limits upon myself. I needed to do something—anything. My desire to be confident and take risks was growing, *burning*, but fear was my faithful sidekick, and fear always had a lot to say. Fear was the creator of my preconceived limits, the voice which told me I wasn't good enough, always asking me with derision, "Who do you think you are?" any time I tried something new—especially if it was big and bold and different from anything I'd ever tried before. Fear was the voice which could enumerate the potential ways I'd fail, framing failure as catastrophic, as *the worst thing.*

Since my friends wouldn't provide any kind of support for my dreams, I scoured the Internet for outdoor retreats. That's when I decided on a week-long retreat in Winter Park, Colorado with Women's Quest—a business run by a former professional triathlete and all her triathlete friends. I found them in the most nondescript way—via Google. The language of their website drew me in, talking about tapping into your heart's desire with adventure to spark your passion and empower you to live life. The retreats were designed for women of all ages and athletic backgrounds. No experience required. And to cap it off, they quoted the poet Mary Oliver: "What do you plan to do with your one wild and precious life?"

This was for me.

There was hiking and yoga and mountain biking. And the ropes course. But the ropes course was supposed to be *optional.* It said so right on the website! I could do everything but the ropes course, I thought, because the ropes course scared the crap out of me. I created an entire list of reasons why I didn't want to do the ropes course.

Not good at climbing.

No upper body strength.

Not brave enough.

I told the staff I wanted to pass on the ropes course, but they talked me into going to the site. (That's where lunch was being served. If I wanted to eat, they explained, I at least needed to go with the group. And, of course, I wanted to eat.) When it came time for high elements on the ropes course, that trusty sidekick of mine—fear—poured on the doubt. There were thirty other women on the trip and all of them seemed like they were fit and fearless and kick-ass and amazing. There were women who were training for a triathlon, women who were natural on a mountain bike, women who had run half-marathons and won 5Ks.

Me? I was only beginning, at age thirty-two, to explore my athletic side. I was an interloper, someone just trying to feel her way through the lingo of running with heart-rate zones and intervals and something called "VO$_2$ max." I felt like a poser, someone who could purchase the gear and put the trip on her credit card, but when it came down to it, was no athlete at all. For example: this ropes course. It was beyond my ability.

Comfort zone? Not even in the same zip code.

Shouldn't I start with something easier?

Already, I was letting my whining get in the way of my inner athlete.

But I'm too fat.

But I'm too inexperienced.

But I'm not strong enough.

But I'm not ready.

But I'm not cool enough.

Here's the thing: I was the only person who thought I was fat and weak. It's a story I told myself over and over again, dating back to junior high. I compared myself with other girls, and I didn't look like other girls. I was thick. My breasts developed, my hips rounded, and my stomach has never, ever, in the history of *ever*, been flat. My thighs, also, were thunderous. I didn't look like the women in the TV commercials for athletic shoes and sports drinks. And because I didn't *look* like them, I thought I couldn't do the amazing things they did.

But here I was, at an athletic retreat in Colorado, being coached by former professional triathletes. I'd already stepped outside of my comfort zone just by following my heart's desire to try something athletic and adventurous. My inner athlete was not going to let me back out so easily. I came here for a challenge. Stubbornness trumped the fear of looking foolish.

It was time to give the ropes course a try.

The "Leap of Faith"—Who was the smart-aleck who came up with *that* name?—seemed to be the most accessible of the high elements for me. It was a thirty-foot-high pole with a small platform and a trapeze bar about ten feet away. The idea was to climb the pole, stand on the platform, and jump to grab the trapeze bar. Climb the pole? Jump? Into the air? What if the ropes broke? What if I couldn't climb all the way up there and got stuck mid-pole? What if the harness malfunctioned? What if I didn't grab the bar? And if I did grab the bar, how would I get down? The many questions, not one with a positive bent, flooded my mind.

But everyone was having such a good time on all the high elements. The staff said very few people ever grabbed the bar; that didn't need to be the goal. The ropes-course specialist said you didn't have to stand up to jump; you could sit on the platform and scooch yourself off the edge. That notion seemed to the deciding factor for a couple of the other women who agreed to give it a try. That seemed doable. Scooching. That didn't sound too hard.

I am here to challenge myself. I am here to be brave. I am here to do something with my one wild and precious life.

I can do this!

The staff helped me into the harness, which pulled unnaturally around my crotch, sat tight around my hips, and generally made my midsection look large, lumpy, and ridiculous.

I can do this!

I put on the bright blue safety helmet and walked over to the pole.

I CAN DO THIS!

. . . and then I started to cry.

The confidence that got me into the harness was fleeting. That positive, encouraging inner athlete was nowhere to be found. My ever-present sidekicks doubt and fear were in control and telling me that I would never, ever make this climb. *You're an overweight power walker who occasionally does yoga,* my doubt and fear told me. *You have never had any upper body strength. How do you expect to climb this pole?*

I started climbing anyway, taking one step up the metal rungs, breathing, then taking the next step. I did OK for a few minutes. Then the rope got tangled with itself. It swung out and knocked out one of the metal rungs above me. Sheer panic set in with a dose of disbelief.

Are you kidding me? How was I supposed to climb when my next step had literally fallen to the ground? *Now* what was I supposed to do?

Diane, a member of the Women's Quest staff, came over and picked the metal rung off the ground.

"Here, Amy. Put it back in."

I was still close enough to the ground where Diane could hand me the fallen metal rung.

This didn't stop me from hyperventilating.

The hyperventilating only grew as I tried to fit the rung back into the pole. It didn't fit.

"I can't do it." Tears were streaming down my face. "I just can't do it. It won't go back in. I broke it. I can't do it."

"Yes, you can, Amy. You have it upside down."

I flipped the rung around. Oh. There. I got it. OK. I took a big breath in. Big breath out.

Here I go.

PLUNK!

The rope got tangled again. It knocked out the metal rung. Again. Someone came over, handed it back to me. This time, at least, I knew how to put it back. I shoved the rung into position. It was a small victory in a fleeting moment, but it ratcheted up my confidence ever so slightly, which helped push the fear away just a tiny bit.

Up I went.

I passed the removable rungs and into the permanent ones. I made progress amid a chorus of grunts. I started to think it through: *Reach with my hand. Pull with my arm. Push with my leg.* I looked where to grab next, where to place my foot.

I was climbing. And still crying. And the crying, I'm sure you can imagine, didn't help the climbing. I paused a minute to assess my position. About halfway up. Only halfway?

For the love of Pete, does this pole ever end?

I didn't know if I could make it much farther.

Making matters worse, my rope kept catching on the rungs. One step, move the rope. Another step, move the rope. It was annoying. Why couldn't I climb smoothly like the rest of the women? But it created a rhythm—step, move the rope; step, move the rope. It became more difficult to pay attention to what fear and doubt were chattering about in my head when I focused on the rhythm of solving this particular problem.

I was near the ledge when I encountered another problem.

How was I supposed to get *on* the ledge?

The rungs were no longer spaced in predictable distances. Some were far apart, others so close together even my small foot couldn't cram into the space to give any leverage. My rhythm was gone. I now hugged the pole, my arms and legs wrapped around, holding on for dear life until I got a better idea. What if I couldn't make it? What would happen then? Would I have to climb back *down*?

Oh God, please no.

But I was stuck. I was stuck and I didn't know how to get out of it. I was afraid—*petrified*—of falling. I feared not completing the task and facing internal humiliation and outward condolences of "Nice job, anyway."

There were about fifteen women on the ground, shouting encouraging words to me. The number around the pole grew as I climbed. They knew, or could sense, this was a challenge for me. And while I was the one pulling myself up this thirty-foot pole, they were still supporting me somehow. Some yelled versions of "You can do it!" while others tried to give me specific directions as I clung to the pole for dear life. It was difficult to understand their words through my panic and tears. My brain was still wondering about climbing back down, but my body knew better. My body apparently *knew* it could do this. I swung my leg around the front . . . up and over the platform. Cheers wafted up from the ground.

I now sat—backward, but *sitting*, dammit—on the platform.

My lungs produced a slight wheezing sound. *Remember to inhale.* I was out of breath. *Deep breaths. In through the nose, out through the mouth.* In one courageous motion, I turn myself around.

Wow.

I am here.

The arduousness of the task faded immediately from my mind and I drank in the view. The Colorado mountains were glorious—tall and strong yet with a gently curved silhouette in every shade of green, popping against the shockingly clear and bright azure sky. The pine trees, tall and straight, were covered in deep, richly colored needles. Color was never as vibrant and crisp as it was in this moment. The height didn't bother me one bit as I looked out at this magnificent view. I was wedged onto this small ledge, but everything felt expansive in that moment. I wanted to sit in this spot for as long as I could. I looked at the view hungrily, almost greedily, but with patience and purpose so as to etch this view, these colors, into my memory for decades to come.

All week long, the group talked about intentions and intention setting. We were told to set an intention at the top before taking that leap of faith and jumping off into the unknown.

But it wasn't the unknown that scared me.

It was that climb. If there was an option to magically be lifted to the platform to take in the view, set an intention, and jump off, I would have been all in. That would have been easy. The scary part, the difficult part, was getting through all those obstacles—the unlucky position of the rope, knocking off the rungs, the crying (which greatly reduced my lung capacity). It was getting through the self-doubt which pestered me at every obstacle, planting thoughts of unworthiness and failure and the possibility of an untimely (and stupid) death. It was taking the cliché "It's the journey and not the destination" and putting it into practice—a practice which would become a way of *living* life, instead of just talking about it.

In this tiny experiment, I was near my destination—completing my leap of faith. The journey was getting to the point of jumping. What did that journey feel like? Terror mixed with triumph. Like my muscles were burning one minute, and in a comfortable rhythm the next. I needed to stop questioning, to stop second-guessing everything I was doing and thinking and feeling and wanting to be. I came to a stop with a breath—a long, deep breath—and looked around the present moment. Once I saw what was in front of me—all my available options, all the strength and smarts I already possessed—I was able move forward.

I was able to surprise myself.

I took one more look at the mountains and the cloudless sky. One more deep breath. I set my intention. This. I wanted more of this. I wanted these challenges and adventures. I wanted these experiences and sights that only come when I push myself out of my comfort zone. I wanted this living, really *living*, my one wild and precious life.

To get here, I fought myself. I cried. I whined. I doubted. The journey wasn't pretty. It was awkward and tear-stained and thick with shallow breaths. But I did it. I sat with a sense of accomplishment, not just of the climb up the pole but of putting myself on a new path, one that would be challenging and twisting and would at times double back on itself. But a path that felt more authentic to the way I wanted to live.

Slowly I wiggled my butt to the end of the platform.

One . . . two . . . *three.*

Suddenly I was falling. The rope caught. My arms flew out.

In an instant it was over. I screamed and then smiled.

The journey wasn't over. It had only just begun.

Creating a Body of Evidence

As we left Winter Park, we were cautioned several times: Do not go home and immediately start making major life decisions.

There is a euphoria that comes from a week of facing fears and insecurities when surrounded by encouraging and inspiring women. You may feel like we could conquer the world, but it's best not to go home and quit your job or leave your husband. Wait two weeks, we were told. Let some time pass between the adrenaline rush of the retreat and the return to everyday life.

The adrenaline rush was real. My inner athlete had been given some room to play in Winter Park and she was starting to develop her own voice, one that countered my trusty sidekick, fear. Occasionally they would argue. Fear was a comfortable voice. Fear tried to keep me safe, both physically and emotionally. Fear wanted me to stay small. Taking chances, *big* chances, might mean pain and failure. Fear wanted to protect me from taking chances.

But my inner athlete tried to reassure that voice of fear. There was nothing we could not handle, she said to my fear. Don't you remember the Leap of Faith? My athletic-self loved the stories the staff of Women's Quest told about triathlons, about the racing and the training and the friendships. The challenge seemed less daunting when they discussed swimming, biking, and running as if it were just one big party where the triumphs were great but the missteps made them laugh even more. Their stories were rarely about success but about training and races gone wrong. That's where the best stuff was. That's where my inner athlete started to question that voice of fear, which tried to avoid mistakes at all costs.

I began to create for myself a history of success, a body of evidence that I could do hard and scary things. I could be athletic. I could make mistakes and still be cheered by the group.

My inner athlete said, "Maybe mistakes aren't so bad after all."

Discovering Opportunities

It was a Saturday morning in North Buffalo and I was at a small corner diner, one with a counter that peered over to the kitchen with a haphazard selection of tables arranged around a row of window booths in an uncomfortable attempt to maximize the seating capacity. My boyfriend spent breakfast running down his latest list of my faults, couched in helpful language of what I *should* be doing and what would be "best" for me.

I frowned and nodded.

In hindsight, this was the beginning of the end of our relationship. I was starting to feel the ways in which he would break me down instead of build me up. I started to notice the other people in my life who were the same way—the people who said hurtful things under the guise "friends should always be honest." It's not that I surrounded myself with bad people. It's that I was surrounded by unsupportive people, friends (and boyfriends) who failed to dream big with me. On my Women's Quest adventure, I met a couple dozen women who would lift me up, encourage me, laugh with me, and give me advice in supportive tones without the condescension.

My inner athlete was starting to emerge in bits and pieces. It became easier for me to question other people's analysis of my life. And it was *my* life. I was growing weary of waiting for the perfect timing, for my boyfriend's change of heart, for something to happen to me instead of created by me.

I frowned and nodded again. He told me to lighten up (a phrase which usually has the opposite effect, making me wallow in my unworthiness even longer) then went to pay the bill. I waited in the tiny vestibule, casually scanning the corkboard filled with everything from hand-printed flyers looking for roommates to professional advertisements for grass-cutting and snow-removal services. There, amid the clutter, was a large poster for the Wilson Wet & Wild Triathlon.

Whoa. Whoa. Whoa.

Wait just one minute. There was a triathlon? Here? In Western New York? People did triathlons *here*? Ordinary people in my hometown did these things? My mind was blown away. I thought triathlons were only in exotic locations. (And much love to Wilson, NY on the shores of Lake Ontario, but exotic it is not.) I thought only mega-athletes did triathlons, that it was out of reach for ordinary, run-of-the-mill, semi-fit girls like me.

I tried to memorize as much as I could, right there and then in the diner.

It was held in early August—which meant the event had already taken place.

The swim was 600 meters.

The bike was twenty miles.

The run was a 5K.

Perhaps this was doable. Well, *maybe* it was. There were some obstacles I needed to tackle first. I didn't know how to swim, so that would be problematic. I had no idea how far 5K was, but it was probably farther than I had ever run before. Twenty miles on a bike sounded like an accessible distance, although I'd need an actual bike and not the cruiser with the hard plastic seat that had been my grandmother's in the 1980s.

Truth be told, these facts made me doubt this sprint triathlon would be achievable for me. But I didn't care about the facts. My heartbeat quickened. My eyes widened. My face broke out into a smile. This was surely a sign to my inner athlete that she could find support right here at home, that she could challenge me where I was. No exotic location or elite-athlete status required.

I pointed the poster out to my boyfriend. He laughed. "You? Do a triathlon? But you'll embarrass yourself," he said.

This time I didn't frown and nod. This time a small smirk of determination crept across my face. I filed away the information and allowed it to simmer in my soul. There were triathlons nearby. This was a possibility.

That's all my inner athlete needed to know.

A Poseur on Two Wheels

You're NUTS!

The voice was faint but unmistakable. It was one of Gram's favorite sayings, one she used anytime anyone did something outside what she considered "the norm"—which meant she said it to me quite often. The whispering voice had the enunciation spot on, with the emphasis on "nuts" slightly drawn out for added impact.

It was a glorious June day, warm but not too hot, a slight breeze, and a blue sky dotted with clouds. I had turned onto a country road, guiding my specialized road bike with confidence. There were some riders ahead of me, but I was on my own at this point, riding steady and strong with a huge smile on my face.

You're NUTS! I heard my grandmother say.

It had been five years since she died—a long time before she decided to make any kind of supernatural contact with me. Maybe it was a figment of my imagination, a connection to her I wanted to have on that day.

But I think she was slightly proud of me and wanted to let me know.

It was my first time participating in the Ride for Roswell, a bicycling event that raised money for Roswell Park Cancer Institute in Buffalo. Gram never went to Roswell for her cancer treatment, but still, I raised money and rode in her memory. It somehow felt appropriate, both as a way to honor her and to celebrate the last two years in which I'd allowed myself to play with this athletic identity and embrace cycling.

My life-affirming decision from Women's Quest was to purchase a proper road bike. It was two weeks after my return when I went to a local bike shop, test rode a few models around the neighborhood, and made the $1,500 investment in a real, honest-to-goodness road bike. In the cycling world, this was a quality but low-end bike. To some of my family and friends it was a frivolous impulse purchase. Part of me tried to explain the freedom I felt on the bike, how riding truly connected me to my inner athlete, gave me time to clear my mind and listen to what she was trying to tell me.

On the bike I had the chance to listen to my heart.

But another part of me felt compelled to justify—even to myself—the expense. After all, who was I to be spending money on good cycling equipment and apparel? I wasn't really an athlete. I just had the disposable income to look like one.

In high school they were called "poseurs"—people who pretended to be what they were not. They would co-opt dress and speech and mannerisms in order to fit in with a particular social group. There's an inauthenticity about it, an insincerity. A poseur is searching for some perceived perk, like popularity or to impress a love interest or to piss off parents. A poseur doesn't *really* want to be part of that culture. A poseur doesn't *really* identify with it on a deeper level. It's a superficial exhibition.

This was my feeling when I arrived for my first group ride with a local cycling club. The ride leader asked about my background. "This is my first group ride," I said. He shook his head. "Well, you *look* the part," he said, with a clear intention of offering me support.

Immediately I deflected. It was my go-to reaction whenever someone paid me a compliment, voiced support, or congratulated me. My knee-jerk reaction had always been to downplay accomplishments or anything remotely looking like skill. *No, no,* I tried to say. *You have the wrong idea.*

The same behavior came out in the parking lot of the group bike ride as I deflected the notion that I looked the part of an actual cyclists. "Anyone can look the part," I said. He smiled uncomfortably, shrugged his shoulders, and walked away.

When he sees me ride, I thought, *he will think I'm a total poseur. Best to quash that right now. Because I want to be a cyclist and an athlete, but I'm afraid when he rides with me and sees my lack of both knowledge and skill he won't be able to control his laughter.*

I signed in, took a copy of the cue sheet with the turn-by-turn directions, and hopped on my bike. I settled into the back of the group for the twenty-mile ride. People asked my name, where I was from, and how I found the group. They gave me tips when they saw I was in the wrong gear. They told me stories about other group rides and gave me suggestions for which ones I might like.

You know what nobody did?

Laugh.

Nobody. Laughed.

I was the second to last person to finish the ride, yet people still thanked me for coming and hoped I would come back again. I was expecting to be judged, expecting to be found out as someone who just gave her credit card a workout to buy some low-level bike gear. I was anticipating the worst, and nowhere near the worst happened.

I left surprised and smiling.

I came back week after week to bike, learning tips and tricks. I was still a novice at using my gears and the other riders helped me learn how to use them. The rides I did were pretty flat, so I didn't learn much about hills, but I did learn about bike safety. My old elementary-school learning about arm signals started to kick in and I became part of the chorus that would yell "Car back!" when a vehicle was approaching alongside our group.

By the time I had registered for the Ride for Roswell, I was easily biking twenty miles at a time. This thirty-three-mile route would be the longest I had ever done.

When I heard Gram's voice say *You're NUTS!* I felt an overwhelming sense of approval.

As I continued the ride, thinking about Gram, a faint recollection emerged. Did she once tell me she was a member of the Polish Falcons gymnastics program when she was a child? Did she once say, with a bit of pride, that she was pretty good on the pommel horse? How did I bury this piece of information? How did I not ask more questions when she was alive and vibrant and in her prime storytelling days?

The tales of tumbling at the Polish Falcons have faded with time, and Gram's achievements went with her to the grave. What's left is the barebones history of the club for Polish-Americans, which was active and popular in my grandmother's youth when it featured an emphasis on physical fitness and physical education. Gymnastics became one of the main activities of the club.

Trying desperately to find out more about gymnastics and the Polish Falcons, I found out that Stan Musial, a member of the National Baseball Hall of Fame, grew up competing in gymnastics at the Polish Falcons in Pennsylvania. He credited tumbling with helping to develop his athleticism, which served him well in a Major League Baseball career that began in 1941 and ended in 1963. Musial was an outfielder with the St. Louis Cardinals, winning three National League Most Valuable Player Awards.

Gram was born in 1921, Musial in 1920. Contemporaries (in terms of living on the planet), they had a shared history of Polish Falcons gymnastics. I've often wondered if she was a Stan Musial fan. Maybe. Maybe not. After all, he didn't play for Buffalo. And Gram's heart was always with Buffalo. Without much of the story, I had only my imagination, fueled by hours on the bike, to create my own stories of Gram's tumbling background.

You're NUTS!

I saw her face as she said it, a twinkle in her eye and a slight upturn of the corners of her mouth. Maybe I was nuts, but I was Gram's kind of crazy.

I finished the thirty-three-mile bike ride feeling tired.

And strong.

And accomplished.

And ready for the next thing.

It was time to test the waters of my emerging athletic identity. Literally.

Chapter 3: Sink or Swim

Baby Strokes

I arrived in downtown Buffalo just before 6 a.m. The city was dark and still, an odd mix of eeriness with a dash of peacefulness. The unusual atmosphere fit my mood, which combined the contradictory feelings of anxiety and excitement, anticipation and dread.

The gym opened at 6 a.m. and it was imperative I arrived early. First was the practical aspect. Not only did it offer the opportunity for a parking space on the street near the door (before the Parking Violations Bureau starts writing tickets for the day), but it ensured that I would get my own lane in the pool. That was key.

When sharing a lane in the pool, flailing and floating on your back is frowned upon.

I gravitated toward the early-morning swims because that's what I thought swimmers did. In college, the swim team practiced ridiculously early. I knew this because I worked on the student newspaper, often pulling all-nighters. The only people at the dining hall when breakfast opened were the newspaper kids and the swimmers. We all shared beleaguered faces, but they had those really cool, warm, ankle-length parkas. Man, those were cool.

Now that I was an aspiring triathlete, I wanted to feel like one of those real swimmers in college. I didn't have the parka, but I could get to the pool at the butt-crack of dawn.

The most important reason, however, for these early-morning swim sessions were so that as few people as possible saw what passed as my "workout."

One other early bird was there cranking out laps like it was his job. Thankfully he ignored me as I took a deep breath and eased into the shallow end. Grasping the side wall, I began my workout. Bending my knees, I plunged myself underwater, blowing air out of my nose and my mouth, and then returned to the surface to take a fresh supply of oxygen. Repeat. This is called bobbing. I did this twenty times.

Next up: Floating. I turned onto my back and floated. The first few times I only lasted about a quarter of a pool length before I turned around and floated back. I worked up to another floating drill on my back where I gently rotated my body from side to side. Eventually, I did this rotation and floating drill with my face in the water.

I was in the water for about twenty minutes.

I felt like an idiot.

I was an adult and I was bobbing and floating in a pool used almost exclusively by actual swimmers who dive in and churn out laps in easy, effortless motions. I would grab for the side wall if water accidentally got up my nose. This is not how swimmers act. And while I knew I needed to practice, that I was starting from zero with no formal training in the water, the bigger part of me was embarrassed by my lack of knowledge and skill. I could fake it on the bike—I had learned to ride as a kid. But in the pool I was completely exposed as the unathletic beginner I felt I was.

Baby strokes, right? I had to learn to swim from scratch.

Growing up, I could expertly perform an underwater handstand (with the assistance of my ever-present nose plugs), summer swimming meant backyard pool games (Marco Polo, anyone?), and yearly outings to The Lake (usually Erie, sometimes Ontario) to try and jump waves and collect shells. There were no formal swimming lessons, but I knew enough to stay afloat. Actual strokes, however, eluded me, and I had no idea how to successfully swim from one spot to another.

When I registered for my first triathlon, this became the crucial detail.

I signed up in November 2007 for the Keuka Lake Triathlon in June 2008. That gave me seven full months to complete my most difficult task—learning how to swim. A local aquatic center offered adult learn-to-swim lessons, which is where I received my bobbing and floating assignments. Eventually I progressed to actual swimming down the length of the pool.

Ah-ha! I thought triumphantly. *I can now swim!*

Progress, however, is rarely linear, as my inner athlete would teach me.

As usual, I arrived downtown at the butt-crack of dawn. I slid into my lane and gently swam down and back. One lap down. Then little things started going wrong. My goggles kept fogging up. I'd lift my head out of the water too high when taking a breath and my lower body would sink. I kept getting a mouthful of water and choking mid-length. I had several false starts, pushing off from the wall, taking one stroke, and turning over onto my back to float back to the start. I couldn't complete another lap. After ten minutes of this, I got out of the pool.

Sitting in the locker room alone, I cried. I sat on a bench, towel wrapped around my wet bathing suit, goggle marks deep around my eyes, and sobbed. I tried to stifle it, but the more you resist crying, the uglier it becomes. Within seconds tears were streaming down my cheeks and my stomach heaved in and out as I gasped for air in a full-body bawl.

Failure. This was a failure. This swim was a failure.

This whole crazy triathlete experiment was a failure.

There was no way, no *way* that I could do this. Who was I to think that I could learn to swim? Who was I to think that I could swim in a *triathlon?* I would *never* be able to do this.

And so I slid further into the downward spiral of doubt. I had completed my adult learn-to-swim course and I still struggled to complete one single length of the pool, let alone one lap ... let alone the 750 meters I would need to swim in Keuka Lake in a few months. I was no longer progressing, I feared, but rather regressing.

It was only 7:30 in the morning and here I was, crawling back into bed, letting the tears continue until I fell back asleep.

How do you go back and try again after what felt like an epic failure?

Turns out, you just go out and try again.

Feeling the Rhythm of the Lane

It was December. There were still six months before my first triathlon.

Six.

Months.

Time was on my side. If it was easy, this journey wouldn't be nearly as important to me as it was. If this journey was easy, I wouldn't really be interested. And if I was to consider myself an athlete, if I was truly going to join that club, I had to embrace failure.

So back to the pool I went.

It wasn't pretty and I spent a lot of time working on drills, but I went back to the pool. I swam a lap. And then I swam another one. A few workouts later I had put together 500 yards. Continuous, without stopping. I exchanged my locker room full-body sobbing for a full-body happy dance. Eventually I worked up to 800 yards—the approximate distance I'd need to swim in the triathlon.

Hey! Did you see that? I can swim! I can swim!

My confidence was growing. At least in the pool, where there was a black line to follow at the bottom, clear water, and lane lines.

Open-water swimming is a completely different animal. The keys I learned in my adult class weren't always useful in the lake. Swimming in the pool was about finding your rhythm and gliding. Swimming in the open water was about finding your stroke as a variety of elements conspired to disrupt your rhythm.

It felt like an entirely different *sport.*

Ten Strokes Out, Ten Strokes Back

It was in October of 2007, at the age of thirty-four, when I met with a triathlon coach to see if it was even possible for me to attempt a triathlon. It took her all of five minutes to assess my situation.

Of *course* I was capable of a triathlon.

I had never run before, not for longer than, say, five minutes, and I didn't know how to swim. The bike part, by this time, I pretty much had down. But that all seemed like minor details to her. She was already plotting what races I could do and creating a training plan that would get me running and cycling with regularity.

When my coach first suggested the Keuka Lake Triathlon on June 8, my brain went like this:

June. Summer. It will be warm, but not too warm.

Sounds good to me.

Ah, but while Western New York summers are fantastic, the weather doesn't really start to warm up significantly until *mid*-June. And as the triathlon started to get closer I realized that training in open water was going to be a challenge. Because you don't jump in Lake Erie in May when water temperatures are only in the mid-fifties.

At least not on purpose.

To my relief, there were other crazy souls training for the Keuka Lake Triathlon who wanted to get in some open-water swims. I joined in on a group swim, showing up with my brand-spanking-new wetsuit.

If learning to swim was challenging, getting my wetsuit on was downright frustrating. You need to tug and pull so the suit is snug all the way up your body, but you need to be gentle so as not to rip it. This was difficult work. And it was awkward. There was no way to do this modestly. I hoped no one was looking, because I looked ridiculous. Finally, I worked the suit up around my waist. Sweat was already pouring down my face from the effort.

I was already *sweating . . .* from putting on *clothing.*

I pulled the suit up my torso and put my arms in the sleeves. One of my fellow triathletes took pity on me and came over to help, grasping the extra neoprene along my arms and tugging it up to give me a snug fit. He pulled up the zipper in the back and *voila!* I was in my wetsuit!

Could. Not. Breathe.

How was I supposed to swim in this?

No, really, how did this work? I asked.

You just swim, the guys told me.

Oh. OK.

The swim site was an old, abandoned commercial slip along Buffalo's outer harbor. The area had fallen into limited use and the triathlon club came here weekly in the roughly 300-meter-long protected slip. The advantage was protection from waves and generally calmer waters than out on the open lake; the disadvantage was that the slip provided a perfect place for debris of all kinds to gather. Lake junk—seaweed, weeds, sticks, leaves—collected in the channel. Dead fish also floated there, some days abundantly, which produced a putrid smell.

While there was some gunk gathered along the wall, there were no dead fish and the water was relatively calm. The guys walked in and started swimming out to the end of the pier.

This was not for me.

Luckily there was one woman, Nancy, who was also there for her first open-water swim. In her fifties, Nancy was an accomplished runner who decided to take up triathlon for a different challenge. We were both scared. So at least I had a partner.

We waded into the water. I put my face under and coldness took my breath away. I kept putting my face in the water, blowing bubbles, floating. Anything to get used to being in the open water. Nancy and I devised a strategy. We would swim out ten strokes. I put my face in the water and, to my surprise, made it all ten strokes. I had veered way off to the right, and I took a breath on every stroke, but I swam ten strokes. We hung out, treaded water, and then did ten strokes back.

Nancy suggested we try twenty strokes this time.

I declined. Nope. No. No. No. Nope. No, thank you. Ten strokes out and back was just plenty for me.

So we did that twice more.

It wasn't smooth. I stopped a few times, choked when I mistimed my stroke and water poured into my mouth and up my nose. For the longest time I tried to fight the movement of the water, tried to impose my will, to move my body across the water with purpose and determination. But mostly my focus was on breathing and staying alive.

The first open-water swim totaled 100 meters at best. I spent more time trying to get my wetsuit on than I did in the lake. I was scared of what this meant for race day. Would I be able to swim in open water? Would I be able to make the entire 750 meters? But also, there was just a hint of happiness. I went out of my comfort zone. *Way* out of my comfort zone. I was too caught up in the details of my pending race to really see it and embrace it, but by facing something hard and scary and doing it anyway, I was beginning to reap the benefits of an athletic identity.

Of course, I downplayed it. This is what I routinely did—take any accomplishment and qualify it. By this point it was such an ingrained part of my identity: I compared myself to others, particularly my worst days to their best days; I saw all the ways I needed to get better, all the faults still left to correct. After that first open-water swim, my head was filled with doubt.

I didn't really swim. Ten strokes out and back is not swimming. Who do I think I am, calling myself a swimmer?

But there was another voice inside me that noted we all have to start somewhere. This was just *my* somewhere. It didn't matter that it came more naturally to others. Didn't matter that others experienced this evolution at younger ages. This was where I was. It was where I wanted to be, where I felt I needed to be. I'd figure out the *why* later.

In the meantime, I would just keep breathing and moving forward.

Crossing the First Finish Line

There was terror throughout my entire being the morning of the Keuka Lake Triathlon.

I said mantras and summoned positive thoughts.

I am strong. I repeated it to myself over and over. *I am strong. I am strong.*

Fear coursed through my veins anyway.

What was I thinking?

I could *not* do this.

I could not *do* this.

I was not an athlete. I certainly was not a triathlete. These people around me all knew what they were doing. They all looked confident and sleek and fit. I had wrestled with my wetsuit, was self-conscious of my thighs, and had, at best, ten strokes of open-water swimming on my resume.

But off I went to the swim start. My wave was the last in the water. It was a blessing to have no one starting behind me, no one swimming over me in an attempt to win an age-group prize. I could take my time—which I did, mostly floating on my back around the 750-meter rectangle course with Ashley, the surfing lifeguard, by my side.

As I landed on shore to the announcement—

"THE LAST SWIMMER IS OUT OF THE WATER!"

—my fear was overtaken by pure euphoria.

It wasn't pretty, but I did it.

I sprinted up to transition and easily found my bike (since it was the only one not out on the course). I stripped out of my wetsuit, strapped on my shoes and my helmet, and pedaled away. I quickly found a groove. I started passing people.

Hey! I was *passing* people!

I felt alive and free as the course rolled for nine miles out and nine miles back.

By the time I reached the run, I was around other triathletes and we all started to wilt as temperatures soared into the eighties for the first time that summer. The 5K felt like a million miles of hot, sticky neverendingness.

I passed one of the members of my local triathlon club who encouraged me.

"Just keep moving forward," he said.

That's all I had to do. Move forward.

Then I saw it.

The glory. The finish line.

I burst into what felt like a sprint . . .

And I crossed the line.

Family and friends surrounded me with smiles and hugs and congratulations.

I was hooked. This was amazing. The difficulty in the swim didn't matter, because I made it. I did it. I actually did a triathlon and I was eager to try again. And again. And again. Something clicked inside of me. There was a freedom to swimming, biking, and running. There was an instant shot of confidence with each finish. My body was getting stronger, leaner. I wanted see what I could do in the next race. And the next one.

Turning Fitness into a Finisher's Medal

That first year I did six sprint distance triathlons. Most of my swims included spending time hanging onto kayaks, getting to know the lifeguards as I crawled from boat to boat. But by September I was able to swim without learning a lifeguard's name. I cut my swim time nearly in half, which seems remarkable until you realize those first races I spent a lot of time chatting with lifeguards and floating on my back anytime panic set in. It's amazing how much faster you can make your way around a swim course when you put your head down and actually swim.

When triathlon season ended, I decided to use my newly obtained fitness to enter a half-marathon: Run for the Grapes in St. Catherines, Ontario. I ran it pretty much on a whim with a friend. I had no idea about pacing, no idea about fueling, and instantly became confused by the 13.1-mile course being marked in kilometers. By this point I knew 5K was 3.1 miles. So how far were we at 12K? I asked my friend for help. I looked at my watch and tried to start running faster.

"Why are trying to pick up the pace?" my friend asked.

"I'm doing horrible!" I replied.

"Why do you think that?" he replied, easily running beside me.

"I'm not even running my 5K pace!" I said.

He gave an encouraging laugh. "No! You're not supposed to run your 5K pace in a half-marathon! You're supposed to be slower."

Oh. Well, what did I know? That put my mind a bit at ease, although my body was starting to hurt.

At the end of the race, they put a big medal around my neck. It was heavy and brassy and I felt as if I had just conquered the world. What a way to cap off my first year as an endurance athlete! When we drove through customs on our way home and the official asked if I had anything to declare, I put on a big smile and said "Just my finisher's medal!"

(Side note: He wasn't as amused as I was. Customs and immigration are no place to joke.)

Back home, I basked in the glory of that medal. I wanted to do more. I wanted to run more. I wanted to do longer triathlons. I wanted to collect more big and beautiful finisher's medals. So I kept entering races. Kept challenging myself. Kept talking about how much I loved triathlon and running. Posting on social media how I was starting to see myself as an endurance athlete.

Then an acquaintance asked me at a sports writing conference if she could go running with me. "Sure," I replied. "But I might be slow for you."

"I'm only running 8:30s these days," she said.

Inside I laughed. I had never run a mile in eight minutes, thirty seconds.

"I'm running about a ten-minute mile," I said.

Her eyes narrowed and her head flinched back.

"Oh," she stammered. "I thought since you do triathlons and run so much, you know, I just . . ."

And then she said it.

"I thought you'd be faster."

That stung. It was the proverbial punch to the gut, the blow that undid what now was two years' worth of work. I had found joy in the training. It was difficult and downright challenging. Swimming continued to be my weakest sport. But I had found a joy in the work. I had found a freedom in the structure of workouts, a way to move my body with purpose. I was doing athletic things. I was *being* an athlete.

"I thought you'd be faster."

The words unraveled the confidence I had gained, the belief that I was no longer a poseur but a bona fide triathlete and runner. I shrugged my shoulders, shoved my hands in my pockets, and mumbled an apology for disappointing her with my pace. I left as quickly as possible, ashamed at my lack of running ability.

My sidekick fear whispered, "I told you so. You're not a real athlete."
I sighed and wondered if my fear was right.

Chapter 4: I Run, But I'm Not a Runner.

Making My Outsides Match My Insides

While my self-doubt was in fine form, my inner athlete—who had finally been allowed to play and explore—was not going to be intimidated by that pesky sidekick, fear. I had an athletic side and I loved it. I kept training, kept racing, kept trying new events and longer distances. Endurance sports had become a way for me to cope with what turned out to be a brutal year.

It was February and I was planning my races for the year when my boyfriend of two years broke up with me and my dad was diagnosed with prostate cancer. That happened on the same day. One fell swoop, as they say.

My boyfriend at this time was a distance runner, someone who supported my training—unlike my previous boyfriend, who openly mocked my goals. When I went out on long runs he would drive out to check on me, carrying extra water and Gatorade with him in case I needed replenishment. He went with me to Montreal when I tackled my ultimate challenge—an Iron Distance race. The non-branded Ironman was a 2.4-mile swim, a 112-mile bike ride, and a 26.2-mile run. He helped things go so smoothly that I rarely talk about my Ironman. There's no drama to the story.

There's no drama to the breakup story, either. I wanted to be in a serious relationship. He didn't. It hurt, a lot, to have someone I chose to love decide he didn't want to be in my life anymore. The pain of a breakup is unavoidable, even if you realize at some level it's for the best.

We had the final conversation in my apartment late at night. The next morning, still gutted and crying, I received a call from my mom. I told her about the breakup. Then she told me her news.

Dad had prostate cancer.

Wait, what?

My boyfriend dumped me and my dad had cancer. I was an emotional train-wreck.

While my grandmother's health issues impacted me, the majority of her diagnosis came too late, when she had already spiraled out of control. This was the first time my parents were impacted by a major health scare. And I had to find a way to cope with it.

His prognosis was good, at least. It was a very early stage and his treatment options were plentiful. I tried to wrap myself around these facts, to snuggle up to them for comfort. The stats were in our favor—and, as a sports-loving family, we were well-versed in the power of favorable stats. My dad, with his usual dose of dry wit, noted, "I figured if you live long enough, eventually you're going to get some kind of cancer." If the diagnosis scared him, he did a fantastic job of hiding it.

While the facts eased my mind, they didn't ease my soul. This was my dad and for the first time in my life I had to face the fact of his mortality. I'd clench my jaw in a desperate attempt to keep the tears forming in my eyes from falling down my cheeks, but it usually was a losing battle. And now, with no boyfriend, no designated partner, to help me process the information and my emotions, I searched for a way to cope.

Endurance sports saved the day. Triathlons and distance running were ways to keep my free time occupied. I was planning and training, scheduling my workouts around work assignments, and often doing two workouts in one day to build a solid base of swimming, biking, and running. And on those long runs and bike rides I was able to just *be*. I didn't have to worry if I was a good enough daughter, if I was doing enough to help my dad and mom through our family's first true health scare. I didn't have to worry about being single at a time when all my friends seemed to be welcoming their second child into the world. All I had to do was just *be*. I was most authentically myself when I was out running or cycling or swimming. And through this time of overwhelming emotion, I needed the physical pain that came with endurance training. My burning lungs and my cramping legs became a cathartic cleansing of the fear and uncertainty that came with my dad's diagnosis.

During that year I searched for races that would challenge me physically. It wasn't about punishing myself, but making my insides match my outsides. And I needed to provide myself with evidence that I could do hard things. So I registered for three races in New York which would be extraordinarily challenging for me: the Sehgahunda Trail Marathon in Letchworth State Park, with around 4,000 feet of climbing and 100 gullies; the Double Mussel in Geneva, which included a sprint triathlon on Saturday and a 70.3-mile triathlon on Sunday; and PAIN in the Alleganies, a 70.3-mile triathlon in Allegany State Park which had a two-loop bike course (which ended up breaking a good portion of the field).

If the races themselves weren't challenging enough, the weather made sure to add a little something extra. While Sehgahunda in May provided few problems, the day of the 70.3 in Geneva brought thunderstorms. Seneca Lake was churning. I was disoriented by the first buoy. The waves pushed me off course—meaning I swam a lot farther than 1.2 miles. By the midway-point of the swim, I thought I was going to throw up. I told this to my mom, who was standing at the swim exit, upon my triumphant return from the lake.

"But you didn't throw up!" she said. "Keep going! Keep going!"

I smiled as I ran into transition to get on my bike. More often, I started listening to the people who were cheering for me, encouraging me to keep going. They weren't drowning out the naysayers—who still chimed in by questioning my slow times and wondering why I would keep going out, race after race, when I wasn't in a respectable position when it came to finishing times and age-group placing—but the encouragers were starting to draw even with the naysayers.

Neither the encouragers nor the naysayers, quite frankly, were much help on the bike ride through the Finger Lakes that day. I rode through thunder-and-lightning storms. I had never been so scared in my life on my bike. Was this safe? Surely some race official would come by and tell me to get off my bike if it weren't safe. I kept on pedaling, using that fear to urge myself to get my butt back to transition and off the bike course, which wound through remote country roads. By the time I hit the run the storms had passed, leaving nothing but heat and humidity and a gross feeling in my legs.

But I finished. And I was healthy.

PAIN in the Alleganies was held in late September; the air temperature was in the 40s with a light drizzle. Red House Lake was warmer than the air—that's how messed up the weather conditions were this day. My swim was the best part of my day.

Let me say that again: My *swim* was the best part of my day. And I'm terrible at the swim.

The bike course is what killed most people. Wet from the swim, I took extra time in transition to dry off and add layers—bike shorts, a dry shirt, and a warm bike jacket over my triathlon suit. I looked slightly ridiculous, but it helped keep me warm. I heard later that at least ten people dropped out of the race during the bike portion with the beginnings of (or maybe just deep concern for) hypothermia.

I survived. The last one to make the bike cutoff. The second-to-last one to finish the run. It was a few days later when I learned I actually won an age-group award—second in my age group. That's how difficult the race had been. I didn't care if I won the coveted award through attrition. I had survived. And that was the point.

I created a year of challenges and tackled them head-on. By the time of my final race, my dad was well on his way to recovery from cancer, folding his radiation treatments into his daily life with few side effects or restrictions. His life was full of normalcy—so much so that most days I forgot he was still a cancer patient.

Relieved at his recovery, I had settled into my endurance training. I faced plenty of doubt and fear. I recognized them well, said hello, and kept moving forward. There were days when I struggled, when I questioned if I was regressing instead of improving, frustrated in the process that was never linear no matter how much I wanted it to be linear. I was in the back of the pack for all three of my major races that year—literally one of the final finishers for each event.

Those near-to-last-place finishes didn't bother me, though. I was out there. I was doing it. I was being an athlete. Right? Even in the midst of doubts on bad days—those days when I couldn't hit my desired minutes-per-mile pace on the run or struggled with the hills on a bike ride or still lacked adequate form on the swim—I still had growing confidence in myself, in embracing the identity of an endurance athlete.

But as my racing drew to a close, I received an email from my friend Erik. He had trained with me for the better part of two years. He was my confidant, one of the people I allowed myself to open to about my fears, about bad training days, about my goals and dreams.

Erik pointed out that I was the second-last finisher at the PAIN in the Alleganies. I was one of the last ten finishers at the Sehgahunda Trail Marathon. Performance was not my strong suit that year. And he didn't know how to tell me this, he wrote, but I was embarrassing myself. If my goal was to write about training and racing and discovering my athletic side, how could I talk about being an athlete when I was struggling, literally, to stay in a race? How could I talk to other people about my experiences when I would just break down and cry? Maybe, he suggested, I should forget about competing and just go hiking instead. Maybe, he told me, competition wasn't for me.

My inner critic was doing a victory dance.

See! You aren't good at this! You're in over your head. You don't have the natural talent to be an athlete. Your times are a joke. Just pack it up, won't you?

But my inner athlete became angry. Didn't Erik understand what the year was about? Didn't he appreciate that performance wasn't everything and that performance could be measured in a variety of ways?

Give up competitive races, huh?

I'll show him.

My decision was to tackle the half-marathon. I knew I didn't have the speed to run an impressive 5K and I was over an hour away from a marathon time which would qualify me for the Boston Marathon, the standard by which so many distance runners measure themselves. The half-marathon seemed like an accessible challenge, a way to show my now former-friend that I could continue to compete even with my slower pace. I could compete with myself and the clock.

And so I set out to clear a popular half-marathon bench mark: run 13.1 miles in less than two hours.

Victory is Mine (And It's Temporary)

It started in Louisville.

The Kentucky Derby Festival Mini-Marathon had been on my racing bucket-list. The "mini-marathon" is actually a half-marathon—though nothing about running 13.1 miles is "mini." The course goes through Churchill Downs, the famed venue which hosts the Kentucky Derby, and really, how cool is that? The race was the weekend before the Kentucky Derby, so the last week in April I loaded up my car—and my playlist—and drove to Kentucky.

I had been training for this race for months. While part of me wanted to show my now ex-friend Erik that I could be "competitive," that I could train to run fast, part of me wanted to show *myself* that even more. Part of me wondered if the previous year's tour of challenging races and basement finishes took away my right to call myself an athlete.

The night before the race, I re-read my training journal. For months I had recorded my daily workouts, writing down what was on my training schedule and what I ended up doing. It included distances and paces with notes about how I felt—sore, tired, amazing, inspired. As I paged through the book, I saw my stats. This was evidence of the work I'd done. I had set a goal—to set a new personal best in the half-marathon—and I had done the work. There was no need to panic. No need to doubt. I had proof that I had trained to run what (for me) would be a fast half-marathon.

The entire morning went smoothly. My early pace was steady but not too fast. The weather was perfect. I cruised through the first part of the course. The turns through Churchill Downs, which took us around the grounds and under the grandstand, gave us views of trainers putting their horses through morning workouts. Some people stopped for pictures. Not me. I left my phone back in my hotel room. I was on a PR (personal record) mission. The time for experience, I thought, was gone. It was all about performance now. This is what Erik was trying to tell me, what he was trying to tell me I lacked. This is what a number of people in the triathlon and running community were telling me. It was time to put up results, they said.

Still, I took time to be in the moment, to let the "cool" factor of running through Churchill Downs course through my veins. I laughed at the college guys from fraternities who had stumbled out onto the streets in the morning to cheer on the runners. I glanced down at my watch. I was on pace for a personal best. Time to giddy up.

After Churchill Downs came the split—marathon runners went one way, half-marathoners another. I truly felt for those people going out, away from the finish line. I know how that feels. I sent them love as I turned to head back toward downtown Louisville.

At Mile 10, one of my fellow runners noted we had just 5K to go. Someone groaned; maybe it was me. It seemed like such a far way to go until the finish line, and the miles were getting tougher. My pace had slowed a bit. My legs were tired. My entire body was tired. It just wanted to be done. But all I had left was a 5K! How many times had I run 5K in my life? How many times had I run 5K in training? Plenty. I just needed to focus. To dig deep. To keep running. I had slowed, but I was still on pace.

Once downtown, it was time to go all-in. I had done this during track workouts, running 400-meter repeats with my core on fire and the faint sensation that I might puke. I drew on that strength and willed my legs to move as fast as they could across the finish line, where I was promptly wrapped in a shiny Mylar blanket. I wound my way through the finishing chute, cutting off people in line to grab a banana and a yogurt. I needed get back to the hotel. I needed my cell phone. I needed to call my mom.

I had just run my half-marathon PR.

Still nine minutes and seven seconds away from the elusive two-hour mark, true—but this was a solid start to the season. I was so elated that I went to the Louisville Bat Museum and had my PR time engraved on a wooden bat. I ate pecan pie and had a mint julep. After a year of grueling races, of beating myself up physically and emotionally, I was back working for specific goals.

A month later, I bested my Louisville time at the Buffalo Half Marathon by forty-four seconds.

Yes! Yes, yes, *yes, yes, YES!*

My work was paying off. My goal-setting was coming together. I was inching toward that sub-two-hour half-marathon. I was brimming with confidence. Victory would be mine, if only in my mind. This was going to be my year.

Until it wasn't.

Falling Apart

After a pair of spring half-marathons, I turned my attention to training for two races in the fall. I envisioned the Mighty Niagara Half Marathon as my triumphant victory lap. After all, I had already set my personal best—*twice*—this year. I expected myself to do it again, right here. The course was flat, with a gentle downhill as it ran along the Niagara River from Lewiston to Youngstown, NY. I was prepared: I'd planned every step of the way, from nutrition to hydration to pace goals.

Best laid plans, as they say.

The only thing that went according to plan was that I got to the start line and crossed the finish line.

I was so obsessed with executing my game-plan that I spiraled into instant anger when the water-stops weren't at the exact mile locations the race's website indicated. Rain made for miserable sections of the run and the slick roads kept me off my target pace. I crossed the finish line, yes, but I was far from amused. I missed my goal time by four minutes. *Four minutes!*

I felt like an utter failure.

I had trained at the pace I needed to run a 2:05 half-marathon, a time which would be my new PR and get me one step closer to that elusive two-hour mark. I had sacrificed for months, keeping my training on track and eschewing any and all junk food, which is not easy in the journalism world where donuts and pizza are the name of the game. I wanted that time so badly. I wanted to prove myself to all the naysayers who wanted me to give up this façade of being an athlete, prove that I was *capable.* I wanted to give them proof in the form of a race result.

But most of all, I wanted that proof for myself.

I refused to give up after just one failure. Redemption, I thought, would surely come a month later at Lucy Town.

Jamestown, NY, is the birthplace of actress Lucille Ball, so the local running club decided to create a half-marathon named after the city's most famous resident. I grew up watching reruns of *I Love Lucy,* so I was thrilled when I learned the finisher's medal was Lucy's face. How could I pass this up? (Also, the first-year event billed itself as a flat course, which was an extra incentive).

What you come to learn about yourself as a runner is that many courses—maybe even most—try to bill themselves as "flat." It may even have been flat to the locals.

It was not flat to me.

Right around Mile 7, I wanted to cry. In the general scheme of things, this is not unusual for me in a half-marathon (I'm sure you've learned that about me by now). At some point in a 13.1-mile race, I will want to cry. Occasionally, I actually *do* cry. On this Sunday, I was again on the brink.

I wasn't anticipating so many hills. Then again, I didn't do much recon work for this one. And while I'd run courses with much more painful climbing, if you're not expecting that particular challenge, it can wreck havoc with your mental game.

That havoc began for me on Mile 1.

The first mile looped through downtown Jamestown, and after a generous downhill I found myself at a big, steep uphill climb.

"Mostly flat," my *ass.*

The course started to even out, becoming less of a hill workout and more of a pretty, rural route. I felt great, working my intervals while staying focused on how I wanted to run. A brief shower dumped about three minutes of rain on us, but the clearing provided a magnificent rainbow, which felt like a blessing from Lucille Ball herself.

I felt OK at Mile 5. Then the mid-course hills started. They were rollers, but more challenging than I was planning on facing. You know how Lucy had that loud, whiny cry? Cue that. Because that is exactly how I felt. By Mile 7, I was in a panic. I wasn't running fast enough. My legs were feeling beat. My running friend Sue had convinced me to abandon my race plan and just run. Forget the PR, she said. Forget time, she said. Just run. I kept running with her and outwardly took her advice, but inside I was still spiraling into disappointment. The last three miles were grueling. It was an endless gradual uphill—with the added bonus (read with heavy sarcasm) of a strong, gusty headwind.

"ARE. YOU. *KIDDING* ME?" I shouted—more than once, I'll admit—announcing my misery to the world (i.e., the other half-marathoners). "This looks *endless!*"

The road stretched in one long, uninteresting line. And I knew what was waiting for us in the last half mile of the course: a long and steep uphill.

Yep. An uphill finish.

By this point I was walking anything that I classified as "steep." Sue had seemed to easily glide up the hill. She kindly waited for me at the top, and while I was grateful for her company and encouragement, I was also hating on myself for not being able to keep up with her. After all, I had talked her into this race in the first place. She didn't even want to come. I was the one who was all "Woo-hoo! Let's run Lucy Town! Watch me, PR!" Now *she* was the one with the enthusiasm and the spring in her legs. I didn't want to hate her, but in the moment I kind of did. There wasn't much left in my legs, but I gave all that I had left to spring across that damn finish line.

One of the volunteers placed the medal around my neck.

I walked away in tears. I walked away from Sue, who had patiently run with me and encouraged me even as I watched my goal slip further and further out of my reach with each passing mile. I left her alone at the finish line. I brushed off my parents, who'd driven two hours to watch me. I couldn't even look them in the eyes, despite their smiles and cheers.

I walked away and cried.

This was not how it was supposed to go. My result did not match my goal in the slightest. It didn't reflect the training I'd done, the work I had put into becoming a better runner, a better athlete overall. I had tried my best and failed. I was devastated.

Even more devastating: I became wrapped up in my results.

I was letting one day define me.

Facing My Inner Critic

At Lucy Town, I ran a 2:12:5. It was my slowest half-marathon in over a year.

On the results page, it didn't look as bad. My time put me 187th out of 374 runners. I was 79th out of 225 females and placed 15th out of 38 in my age group.

What that should have told me was that it was a tough race for *everyone*, both from a course perspective and a weather perspective with the humidity and brief rain shower. But in the moment my mind only listened to my inner critic, the voice of fear that told me I had failed. Maybe my former-friend Erik was right, I told myself. Maybe I should give up racing all together. I was never going to be able to run a sub-two-hour half-marathon. I'd never even get close. What was I doing out here? I was putting in so much effort. I was eating right and hydrating and doing speed workouts. I was doing everything I could and yet on race-day I could never seem to bring it all together. I could never execute. I failed at performance. And wasn't this what being an athlete was all about—

performance? Wasn't success about what you were going to do next? About setting and then reaching big, bold, audacious goals?

My inner critic was doing a happy-dance, and I could no longer hear the voice of my inner athlete. I was in need of an intervention.

Tough Love

We were in her Subaru, driving through the mountains of beautiful upstate New York on our way to Lake Placid for the day. Tara and I met during the infancy of our careers working at the small, locally-owned *Times Herald* in Olean, NY, straight out of our St. Bonaventure undergraduate days. She was a talented photographer while I was a sports writer. Life took us in different directions—me, to Buffalo to continue in journalism; her, to become a staff photographer at a university in the northernmost part of the state. We reconnected one summer when I was walking around the swim-start on Seneca Lake for Musselman 70.3, a half-Iron Distance race, looking for a place to throw up. I heard someone call my college nickname, turned around, and there was Tara. She was watching her friends race and was considering doing a long-distance triathlon herself. (Spoiler alert: She would become an Ironman a few years after that. Granted, she had been a competitive swimmer in high school, but still, the whimsy with which she approached wanting to try an Ironman was slightly insane and something I completely related to.)

We rekindled our friendship over the joys and agonies of triathlon. We talked about our training and about events on our race bucket-lists. We discussed different fueling strategies during long runs, from getting enough water to trying to find energy-gels which didn't turn our stomachs. We celebrated each other's triumphs and laughed as we compared notes on how to pee in the woods during a trail run.

On this particular day, during a late-summer vacation visit I made to the Adirondacks, she needed to lay some truth on me. It came while we were in the car, because all important conversations, it seems, happen in the car. Perhaps because it helps you avoid direct eye contact.

I had been struggling with my run performance, desperately trying to break the two-hour mark in a half-marathon. All I could see was a miserable failure. All I could feel was the frustration of not hitting my two-hour goal and the tears stinging at the finish line. All I could think was whether or not I was truly worthy of calling myself an athlete.

Tara had reached her breaking point listening to this self-deprecation. She offered me her observations with conviction but with love. It went something like this:

"I don't understand why you are so hard on yourself, Amy. I thought when you did the Ironman you would finally be confident. How did that not make you confident? YOU. DID. AN. IRONMAN. Do you ever stop to think about that? You know, I wanted to go sub-two-hours in the half-marathon, too. And I did it. But it sucked. As I was doing it, I realized I never wanted to run in this much pain again. Was running two minutes faster really worth it? Probably not. So why are you beating yourself up instead? You do amazing things, and I think you just don't see the big picture."

I was silent. Words are hard to form when you're choking back tears. Tara was spot-on. I gave myself minimal credit for accomplishments and tormented myself for perceived failures and for not being "good enough" to be an actual athlete.

I had forgotten the good parts of being an athlete. I had forgotten about what it was like when I was first starting out, unsure I could run for any length of time.

It was time to remember.

Searching for My Definition of "Athlete"

I remember a time on the treadmill at the gym with my iPod on shuffle. I started to run when the song "Stronger" by Brittney Spears came on. I decided to run as long as I could. I kept running. And running. And soon enough the song had finished. I ran the entire length of the song.

I looked around the gym. Did anyone see that? Did they? I just ran continuously for an entire Brittney Spears song. Continuous—without stopping!

I was so elated I literally raised my hands in victory.

Somewhere along the way, I lost this type of joy. I became swept up in how some people displayed themselves as athletes. I watched their social-media posts and listened to the way they talked at races and training events. They posted their times; they proudly shared their age-group wins; they based their athletic identity on *results.*

And so I naturally began to apply these standards and definitions to myself. To be an athlete meant *results* and *performance.* That's what my mind said. That's what was being reinforced to me through fellow runners and the omnipresent Motivational Monday memes which stressed hard work as the cure-all for achieving your dreams with catchy phrases like "Dreams don't work unless you do" or "The difference between ordinary and extraordinary is just that little extra."

I was willing to work hard. Hell, I *was* working hard. But I started listening to a universal definition of what it means to be an athlete instead of listening to what my inner athlete really wanted in the first place.

After the truth Tara laid on me that late-summer day, I started to tune in and listen to that athletic voice. Athletic Amy didn't care about a sub-two-hour marathon. Not really. She wanted to be challenged for sure. But she didn't want to be defined only by results. She wanted to train and race and play, and if everything came together for the perfect day, well, all the better. But my inner athlete didn't want to come out only to get results. She wanted to teach me to be brave. She wanted me to see how strong I was today and how strong I was becoming. She wanted me to see how I was putting artificial limits and artificial expectations on myself and how both could keep me living small when what I wanted was to live *big.*

I began training myself to pay more attention to the way I talked to myself and about myself. I also listened to how other runners and triathletes talked about themselves—especially the women. Then I started to notice patterns.

Sometimes it showed as self-deprecating humor; sometimes it was done with an air of humility. It didn't matter the reason or rationale—it was downplaying accomplishments. It was qualifying an identity so deeply important, we were embarrassed to fully claim it as our own.

It often sounds like this:

"I run, but I'm not a runner."

"I'm athletic, but I'm not an athlete."

"Oh, I'm not as good as [insert anyone's name here]."

"I'm too old to be an athlete."

I've said those things to myself, and about myself, many times, and I've overheard many others saying those things about themselves as well. I've heard people say how slow and disappointed they were with their four-hour-thirty-minute marathon.

Um, hey dude, my personal best is 4:45 and I worked my ass off to get that! I would do *cartwheels* with a 4:30 marathon!

Then it occurred to me as I bemoaned my own 4:45-marathon PR that it would be an amazing time to someone struggling to make a six-hour cutoff. Sure, I was disappointed in not reaching those lofty half-marathon goals I set for myself, but I did the work and I did my best; with this new way of looking at running achievements, I shattered some preconceived notions I had about myself, about how strong I was and how fast I could run.

Sure, I wanted to run faster, but that's not the only measure of success.

Finding "Good Enough"

One day, as I was on a twenty-mile run during a period of marathon training, my mom left me a voicemail.

"I hope you had a good run," she said, "but you can take your twenty-miler. I just walked a mile today!"

This was a bit of trash-talking from my mom. Good for me that I ran twenty miles, but for her, walking even one mile was an accomplishment on par with any marathon or personal record I've set. My mom has lung issues from a lifetime of smoking. She quit, thanks to a bout of pneumonia that landed her in the hospital for a week, but her struggles remain. And those struggles help me keep my athletic goals in perspective.

Registering for races—that ongoing competition of trying to best my previous time—is a way for me to structure my training, to kick my rear in gear on the days when I'm just not sure I want to go out for a run. But the competition, the result, wasn't what made me feel like an athlete.

Tara was right. I was missing perspective.

For all the positive things my athletic lifestyle brought me—new friends, the ability to take on challenges, gaining strength both physically and mentally—it was the *negative* I gave the most weight to.

The echo of "I thought you'd be faster" rang in my head. There was this idea among some friends and acquaintances that, because I ran all the time, because I loved to train and race, I must be good at it. And by "good at it" they meant "fast"—even if they didn't know what fast meant. More than once, I've had a conversation with someone who assumed I had qualified for the Boston Marathon. "But you run so much," a casual friend had said to me. "I just assumed you would have run Boston."

Yes. He thought I would have been faster. Not that he meant anything negative by it, but the assumption and my failure to live up to that assumption sounded to me the sum of failure.

There seemed to be no shortage of negative voices chiming in with their opinions. When I first started training, I wrote a public blog about my training experiences and was derided by one fellow (who hid behind a screen name) for training for a marathon. "You should learn how to run a decent 5K-time first," he wrote in the comments section. "Why are you trying to run a marathon when you can't even run a decent 5K?"

After my first year of training, people would comment, "Oh, you're still trying to do triathlons? Well, isn't that nice," as if they were patting me on the head. No one ever *actually* patted me on the head, but they might as well have with all the condescension I felt dripping from their words.

To a small but vocal group of people, I wasn't an athlete. To a small but vocal group of friends and supporters, I was treated as an interloper—cute at best; embarrassing at worst.

Yet somehow, their voices were the ones I heard the most, the voices I gravitated toward when replaying my athletic life in my head. Those negative, brutal, just plain mean voices confirmed the deepest, darkest whisperings of my own fear and doubt. Listening to them gave me an excuse to shrink, to be small and question the voice of my inner athlete. It was so easy to prove the naysayers right. It felt so risky to commit to my inner athlete when I wasn't certain I was good enough, when I wasn't measuring up on the stat sheet.

Turns out, I am not an island. There are others who wonder if they're good enough to claim the mantle of "athlete." Some of them are even Olympic gold medalists.

Read that last sentence again.

Some of them are even Olympic gold medalists.

And I've learned it's not just in the athletic world that the fear of being found out a fake exists. It is all over the creative world—artists, musicians, poets, writers. Which is why when I listened to a podcast by writer Elizabeth Gilbert while in my car (and yes, it made me cry).

Gilbert is most well-known for her book *Eat, Pray, Love,* but in 2015 she wrote the book *Big Magic: Creative Living Beyond Fear* in order to explore the idea of creativity. Not satisfied simply writing about it (as if writing a book is anything but simple—trust me), Gilbert decided to do a podcast series, called Magic Lessons, in which she would help listeners work through their creative blocks.

In the second season, she was helping a poet named Hope who was afraid to put her work out into the world for fear of how it would be received. Gilbert talked with her special guest for the episode, writer and speaker Martha Beck, who had plenty to say on the topic.

"People keep looking for somebody to confirm for them the very worst version of their idea of themselves," Beck said. There might a hundred people who praise her work, for example, but "I can only hear the one who degrades it because I need the confirmation of the darkest, worst voice inside of me that tells me that I'm unworthy and I'm a failure and I'm a fraud. And now it's been proven because some guy Doug at the poetry slam said so. Or—once you get to a certain level—because *The New York Review of Books* said so or *The Paris Review* said so."

Then Gilbert drops the ultimate question:

"Who gets to decide if she's a poet?"

Whoa. I was driving with tears streaming down my face out of recognition.

Yes! That's me!

I keep listening to the one person who questions my athletic pursuits instead of the hundred people who cheer me on. And it got me thinking, who gets to decide if I'm an athlete?

Ideally the answer is me. I am the only one who gets to decide who I am. I am the only one who can claim or reject "athlete." That's my essential self, my internal compass which guides me and allows me to create, whether it's a piece of writing, an Instagram photo, or a track workout.

But my essential self has a nemesis. The social self—the part of me that negotiates society's expectations and structures and is influenced by family, friends, coaches, teachers, media.

There can be a struggle between the essential self and the social self, especially when an identity I want to claim doesn't line up with social expectations.

And there are plenty of social expectations when it comes to being an athlete.

As the external criticism confirms my internal doubts, I become defensive and attempt to justify why I'm training if I'm not winning awards or trying to qualify for the Boston Marathon or at least setting personal bests. "What's the point?" my critics (and sometimes seemingly well-intentioned friends) ask me.

And I get tired of justifying my 5K time. I get tired of explaining why I broke down in the final third of the marathon. I get tired of saying, "Yes, I'm still swimming even though I'm slow and have terrible form!"

On that *Magic Lessons* podcast (Episode 209: "Show Up Before You're Ready") with Elizabeth Gilbert, writer Glennon Doyle Melton said that people "quit because they can't handle defending the thing, which was never their job."

Take a moment to breathe that in.

It is not my job to justify why I train and race. It is only my job to do the work that calls to me, that lights me up, that makes me feel energized and alive. This way of thinking, of looking at my athletic self, was the path to pure freedom. My heart felt as if it were literally leaping for joy. I spent so much time answering the question that fear and doubt posed to me—*Who do you think you are to be an athlete?*—that it never occurred to me that there was a sassy yet poignant answer: *Who am I NOT to think I'm an athlete?* Finally, it struck me that *I* get to define who and what I am. *I* get to claim identities for myself.

Here I was, an adult-onset athlete who was doing some pretty cool things, yet I was dismissing and diminishing my athletic self—my *essential* self. And what's more, other people were doing the same thing. Other women were downplaying themselves athletically. Sometimes it was because they had been collegiate athletes, competing on teams with regimented schedules that placed training on the top of their priority list; since they were now no longer at that elite, focused level, they believed they were no longer athletes. Some took up their sport, running or triathlon or what have you, later in life and felt they were too old and slow to take the title of "athlete"; they were just "trying to stay in shape," as if avoiding atrophy and the desire to live a healthy, active life weren't worthy of calling oneself an athlete. Others didn't think they qualified because they weren't competing—rather, they were climbing mountains or hiking; they cross-country skied and ran for fun, but if there wasn't a race, if competition wasn't involved, then nope, sorry, I may be athletic but I'm no athlete.

The more I heard, the more it bothered me. I mean, wait a minute, you've climbed a *third* of the high peaks in the Adirondacks—how the hell are you not an athlete? You've done several Ironman races, so just because you're not training for one at the moment means you're not an athlete?

Your supposedly slow and embarrassing 5K is faster than I could ever hope to run without the assistance of some motorized vehicle or actual steroids.

How are you not an athlete?

The more I heard, the more I started to check my own self-talk. I was downplaying my accomplishments as a way to justify my joy. Training brought me joy: there was something I loved about having races on my schedule, about getting out and doing the work; there was something I loved about moving my body with purpose, something about the intangibles that came with being an athlete, even if it was in secret.

There was so much I gained when I talked to myself as an athlete. I found ways to tap into confidence and strength. I found peace of mind by moving my body, some days through a gentle pace and other days through a strenuous track-session. I discovered that progress was not linear, that navigating bumps and potholes is part of the journey. I learned that my best stories came from when everything went wrong, not from races that were perfectly fine and uneventful. But still for nearly six years—through marathons, an Ironman, and everything in between—I felt I needed to justify my athletic resume and its results.

It was time to investigate what was holding me, and so many others, back from embracing the identity of "athlete" and discover the power of claiming and naming myself.

Chapter 5: Owning Who You Are and What You Do

Defining a Runner

The more I trained for triathlon and distance running, the more I wanted to learn about other people—especially other women—who were living the life of an endurance athlete. I wanted to know what they did for workouts, for recovery, for nutrition. I was inspired by what they did, how they tackled big things, how they lived lives that seemed like one big amazing adventure. They gave me motivation when I questioned my own desire to live a big athletic life.

But when the opportunity arose to interview some of these women for a variety of work projects, I learned that everyone—even the most badass ultrarunner—has doubts about their athletic identity.

Distance running is an intensely personal pursuit for Krissy Moehl. But the first thing that grabs your attention about ultrarunners isn't their personal stories—it's their insane resume. Interview preparation includes scouring the resume, and that was the first thing I did, spending most of my time picking my jaw up off the floor while reading through her races and results. Krissy has smashed everything from 50Ks to 100-mile races. In 2005 she became the youngest woman to complete what's called the Grand Slam of Ultrarunning—running the Western States 100, the Vermont 100 Mile Endurance Run, the Leadville Trail 100, and the Wasatch Front 100 Mile Endurance Run in the same year. For good measure, she won the Vermont 100.

These are distances I can't even fathom running, let alone running fast, let alone multiple times in a year. And yet, it was quite a journey for Krissy—the record-setting, sponsored, professional runner—to feel comfortable calling herself a "runner."

Krissy's introduction to trail- and ultrarunning came while working at a running store in her native Washington State. As is often the culture of the local running store, group runs become loosely organized, and Krissy—former track athlete at the University of Washington—found herself falling in love with trails and long distances. Soon enough, she was competing—and winning—some of the toughest races out there. Along with that Grand Slam in 2005, she has a number of first-place finishes to her name, including setting the women's-course record at the Hardrock Hundred Mile Endurance Run in 2007 and the Ultra-Trail du Mont-Blanc in 2009. For sixteen years, she competed in ultra-distance races with her running family. And while the distances and the results and resume-building are great, these grueling races over a hundred miles draw Krissy in large part because they are where she feels most vulnerable, most raw. Running is where her physical and emotional passions meet.

"I feel it's a connection I have with the movement," Krissy said. "People ask, 'How do you run for that long?'—and to be completely upfront, I love running. If I don't do it, I don't feel right. It's an emotional attachment and a physical attachment."

Here is what Krissy faces physically on those 100-mile courses: ascents of thousands of feet on mountain trails that require runners to ford streams and rivers, deal with a variety of weather (snow to blazing heat), and do it all through both day and night. The best runners have breakdowns, physical and emotional. It's part of the territory, even part of the draw, for ultrarunners. Krissy's support crew for those races were always fellow ultrarunners. The support crew tends to her physical needs (having her nutrition and hydration at the ready while tending to any physical ailments like blisters or muscle cramps) and her mental needs (helping her dig deep emotionally when her body no longer wants to carry on). With fellow ultrarunners serving these roles, they had intimate knowledge of what Krissy was going through. They understood what a hundred miles could do to the body and to the mind. They could relate.

Her family, however, had no idea what she actually looked like, what she actually went through, during those one hundred miles of running. So in 2016, Krissy decided to change up her crew. She invited four people who had no personal experience with running to be vital support staff, including her boyfriend and her sister.

"I wanted to let them into something that was a big part of my life, and yet they hadn't been privy to it," Krissy said. "I got to share that with them."

Sharing that also meant opening herself up. Ultrarunning isn't glamorous. It's dirty and sweaty and grueling. Her fellow ultrarunners understood the breakdowns, both physical and emotional. All of her doubts and fears, anything that otherwise is easily stuffed away, would be on full display as the grueling miles strip away a runner's façade. But how would her family and boyfriend feel about her after seeing the entire process play out?

"Afterward, something came up with the whole vulnerability of exposing myself, especially with my boyfriend," Krissy said. "It was a vulnerable moment. The day after we got home from the race, I was like, 'Holy cow, you just saw what I'm capable of. You saw me naked in the parking lot, pushing myself when my body was telling me otherwise. All very not-feminine traits. Oh my gosh, are you still going to like me?'

"It was weird. I know I see other people push themselves like that and I'm inspired by it. But in that moment, flipped the other way, I wondered after that how I was being perceived."

In that post-race moment, both her sister and her boyfriend challenged Krissy. She runs races and has sponsors. She coaches. She speaks. She wrote a book, *Running Your First Ultra: Customizable Training Plans for Your First 50K to 100-Mile Race* to help people train for their first ultramarathon.

Now was she finally ready to call herself a runner?

"My sister and boyfriend both challenged me to own what I am and what I do," Krissy said. "When they've seen me in general circles and people ask what I do, I stumble all over my words and stammer out something like 'I do stuff with running.' "

Even the elite runner has difficult calling herself that, claiming the title "athlete."

"I have trouble calling myself a professional runner, even though my income is based on the fact that I coach and race and am a race director. To give a ninety-second speech about what I do is actually the hardest thing I do.

"Initially, I think, the big part was, why do I get to be the one who lives this dream lifestyle? I think it's super cool. Why am I the one gets to do it? I had to justify why I got to do it.

"Now I know I work hard for it. I work harder now than I did in an office. I put in way more hours. If that's how you qualify justification for something."

Krissy is going about doing the earnest work.

"I'm working on owning who I am and what I do."

Owning who I am and what I do. That sounds just like the journey I was on, the one which took me from being *around* sports to be an athlete myself. I needed to own that I was an athlete. I needed to own that I did triathlons and distance running.

I needed to own my own identity.

Why was this so difficult? In part, because my definition of "athlete" didn't match with society's definition of "athlete."

I needed to unpack the definition of "athlete" to discover my assumptions and connect with what I wanted my athletic identity to look like.

Redefining "Athlete"

You might think someone with the title "Queen of Pain" would have a badass definition of what it means to be an athlete.

Not so.

Rebecca Rusch—dubbed the Queen of Pain for her domination of grueling mountain-bike races and her multiple world championships—has more of a broad definition of what makes someone an athlete.

"To me, it's somebody that uses their body as a tool. They have a purpose. Their body isn't just carrying them around to get in the car," Rebecca told me. "Their body is taking them places—to climb a mountain or run a 10K or go see what's around the next corner on their bike. Our body is a wonderful tool that wasn't meant to sit in a chair. So to me, an athlete is somebody using their body to explore and discover and sweat and do something other than just move from place to place around our home and office."

This was an amazingly generous definition of "athlete" from a woman who has made a living as a professional mountain-biker. It sounded spot-on with what I was trying to achieve in my own life; it sang in harmony with the tune my inner athlete had been humming for years.

But it's not the popular definition of an athlete. Diving into the social identity of athletes, research suggests we frame our definition of athletes in very specific ways, created by what we learn from teammates and coaches and what we read and hear and see about athletes in the media.

In 1991, researchers Robert Hughes and Jay Coakley published their academic paper on the sport ethic, *Positive Deviance Among Athletes: The Implications of Overconformance to the Sport Ethic.* In it, they identified core principles of the sport ethic which defined athletes as having complete dedication to the game, being fully committed, and making sacrifices; as striving for perfection with winning an important marker of achievement; and as focused on defying odds and overcoming obstacles that come between them and pursuing their sport.

Nowhere is there a mention of *trying* or *moving with purpose* or *exploring and discovering.* Nowhere is there a mention of *joy* or *love* or *embracing failure.*

Noble efforts are not part of the sport ethic.

They are not part of the definition of an athlete.

We stumble to see ourselves as athletes if we don't fit in with the sport-ethic principles. Our definition, which can encompass high-schoolers to professionals, is narrowed in focus. If winning is an important marker of achievement, then how can a back-of-the-pack marathoner even tiptoe around the identity of "athlete"? If a triathlete cuts a training day short to see family and friends, where's the dedication? Feeling under the weather? If you were serious about being an athlete, you'd be doing your workout anyway.

In conversations with women about what makes someone an athlete, versions of the sport ethic continually come up. Athletes are viewed as completely dedicated and committed to their training—it's their full-time job. They make sacrifices—not just with their body but with their family and friends. And they win. There is no space for losers in the sport ethic or definition of an athlete.

And it seemed that the sport ethic was suffocating my inner athlete.

Fully Committed

To be an athlete means you live the life of an athlete—you're dedicated 24/7 to the pursuit of your goal, whether that be winning the Stanley Cup, an Olympic gold medal, or qualifying for the Boston Marathon. At least that's what the sport ethic tells us when it describes athletes as *fully committed* and *willing to make sacrifices.*

And while I had other important things in my life (work, family) and other pursuits I enjoyed (reading, going to museums) my workouts were scheduled first. I crafted a life where I never missed a swim, bike, or run. Most of the time this brought me joy. But it could also bring me stress.

The alarm would sound at 4:45 a.m. twice a week, usually only four hours after I crawled into bed for a quick, hard sleep. The night before I'd worked a copyediting shift in the office—which meant getting home between midnight and 1 a.m.—but I needed to get to masters swim practice, which started at 5:45 a.m.

In college we had a saying: "Sleep is for the weak." I tried to tell myself that swimming was more important than sleep. I needed the practice. I needed the structure. I needed help in trying to swim in a straight line and to build up my endurance so I didn't have to chat with every volunteer on a kayak along a 750-meter course.

Masters swim was the idea of my triathlon coach, who thought it would help me grow both technically and in confidence. "Masters" is a bit of a misnomer. I associate it with "mastery," but really it has to do with age, and in swimming it just means people over the age of eighteen. This masters swim group had different levels grouped by ability, mostly by how fast you could swim one hundred meters.

I needed to use flippers to keep up with the slow group.

We didn't get much instruction, just in our workouts which varied by group. Frankly, it was intimidating. Other swimmers in my lane kept asking when I was going to ditch the flippers.

Um. Never.

When was I going to do a flip turn?

Um. Never.

But I cranked out the laps as best as I could, even at my slow pace. And usually I was cranking them out on just a few hours of sleep. I didn't feel like I was getting better at swimming, but at least I was swimming consistently, I reasoned. At some point, that consistency had to pay off in performance, right? I was dedicated. I never missed a swim practice, fearful that I would regress in my novice skill-level and unsure what it would mean for me on race day if I skipped a workout. Sleep was a secondary luxury, a sacrifice I was willing to make if it would get me to my end-goal of feeling strong and confident in introducing myself as a triathlete.

After a year of this process, my coach decided I should ditch masters swimming.

"All it does," she said, "is make you sleep-deprived."

A small part of me was relieved, but it battled with the part that was disappointed. It was another opportunity to validate my doubts that I wasn't good enough—not *really*—to be an athlete. *See? You can't hack early-morning swim practices AND you're the slowest in the slow group with no hope of getting any faster.* I had failed a dedication test. I felt a familiar feeling—that of a poseur, of being a fraud.

So it struck me when Robin Valeri said she, too, felt like a fraud. A psychology professor at St. Bonaventure University in southwestern New York State, Robin is cautious about calling herself an athlete—even though she has three Ironman finishes to her name.

Her athlete origin-story sounded familiar to me: Robin is another woman who took up running as an adult. Robin grew up in Westerly, RI, where high-school football ruled the sports scene and she, as a female, was never encouraged to play sports. Her mother did make sure she learned how to swim (they lived near the ocean) and she and her friends rode their bikes everywhere, but never was the activity viewed in an athletic manner.

In college, she took up running and eventually found her way to triathlon.

"I like pushing myself or testing myself," Robin said. "I like the challenge of doing a 5K or a 10K faster, or even a race at an Ironman-level faster."

It's a lure that's familiar for many women. How far can I go? How fast can I go? Can I beat my previous time? Can I work my way up the age-group standings? It's what drove Robin to continue to train and race and complete the first of her three Ironman races in 2009.

"When I did my first Ironman, it was like, 'Wow, I did that,' " Robin said. "I think especially because I grew up and no one ever considered me an athlete. None of my phys-ed teachers said, 'You should go out for volleyball or run track.' To me, this is an amazing thing. But an athlete? I don't know. I guess I'm still not that good at it. I'm not living these things. When someone asks I'll say, 'Oh yeah, I did it,' and add a line like, 'I'm not winning these things.' I would say I'm athletic. I guess I'm uncomfortable calling myself an athlete. It's fun to do, and when I was doing them it certainly was part of my identity. I like triathlon and I'm very proud of it. I'm looking forward to doing that again and having it become part of 'This is who I am.' But I'm not doing anything right now and I feel a little bit like a fraud."

Despite her accomplishments, Robin balks at calling herself an athlete because she's not "living these things" or "winning" or actively training for a race at the moment. Her dedication to the sport comes when she's preparing for a particular race, and then and only then might she see herself as an athlete.

But is athletic identity tied to what you accomplish? Or could your athletic identity be an expression of who you are?

As I dove into the endurance-sport world, I did things which made me feel like an athlete. I had a training plan, with specific workouts and goals, which was much different from the vague activity of "exercise." But did that mean I wasn't an athlete on rest-days? What about when I missed some workouts because I was sick, or the time I had to stop running as I dealt with a bout of plantar fasciitis in my right foot?

Were Robin and I only athletes when we were training?

My inner athlete knew the answer. She was trying to shout it at me, that being an athlete is part of who I am. Running, biking, and swimming along with hiking, strength training, and yoga—these are all *expressions* of my athletic identity, not the *definition* of it. But in trying to define my athletic identity, I had to face my biggest mental obstacle—using results as the measure of success.

Winning as an Achievement

Everyone was yelling at me.

"GET ACROSS! AMY! GET ACROSS!"

What? What are they yelling? What do they want me to do?

I was confused. And tired. And cold. I had just gotten off bike after riding the fifty-six-mile course in Allegany State Park for the PAIN in the Alleganies Half Iron Distance triathlon. The air temperature on this late September day was only in the forties. I was wet from the swim in Red House Lake, and the hilly course hadn't helped. While I generated plenty of heat on the long, grinding six-mile climbs, the downhills were equally long and fast, chilling me to the bone and freezing some of my other fellow triathletes into a DNF (Did Not Finish) after suffering the early stages of hyperthermia.

But I made it, didn't I? Not only did I survive the hellish course under arduous circumstances, but I made the time cutoff, right? What were my friends yelling about?

"THE TIMING MAT! AMY! YOU NEED TO GET ACROSS THE TIMING MAT!"

Crap! In an instant my brain turned back on. I hadn't officially made the cutoff yet—not until I crossed the timing mat. I ran my bike across the mat and into the transition area. I looked back at the race official, who gave me the thumbs-up.

One second.

I made the bike cutoff with one second to spare.

I wasn't just a run-of-the-mill, back-of-the-pack-er. I *was* the back of the pack. I was the last official finisher on the bike and was the second-to-last overall finisher after the 13.1-mile run. But thanks to weather conditions and the impact they had on attrition during the race, I ended up with the second-place award in my age group.

Sometimes the combination of stubbornness with showing up has its perks. And this one came in a red brick award and a jar of almond butter.

It didn't occur to me to be embarrassed by my time until my friend Erik (remember this purveyor of sage advice?), well, flat-out called it "embarrassing."

But here's the thing: sure, I was the back of the pack. I was usually in the back of the pack, on good days I was in the middle of the pack, and occasionally my mid-to-back-of-the-pack time at one event actually gave me an age-group award in another. "Winning" certainly was arbitrary, depending upon who else showed up for that particular race.

Still, it can be difficult to be in the back of the pack . . . because there are tried-and-true back-of-the-pack haters.

If part of the way the sport ethic defines an athlete is through *winning*, then the majority of us who train for the challenge are athletic frauds. While there were inklings from some of the runners I met that what I was doing was "cute" but not "real running," exploring message boards and comments on running stories showed a very vocal group of people who felt slow runners were ruining the sport.

The conflict sharply materialized in a *New York Times* article in October 2009, headlined: "Plodders Have a Place, But Is It In a Marathon?"

My athletic-endurance resume was only two years old at this point, and I was still searching to connect with my inner athlete, but there was still a disconnect. And this debate solidified that disconnect—I felt I was working hard and training and honoring my inner athlete but was being dismissed by a small (but very vocal) group of fellow runners who thought I wasn't worthy of the starting line.

Reporter Juliet Macur set it up this way in *The Times*:

Slow runners "receive a finisher's medal just like every other participant. Having traversed the same route as the fleeter-footed runners—perhaps in twice the amount of time—they get to call themselves marathoners." But hard-core runners felt that was merely participation, not racing, and that slow runners have disrespected the distance and ruined the mystique and majesty of the marathon.

The article quotes Adrienne Wald, then the women's cross-country coach at the College of New Rochelle, who ran her first marathon in 1984, saying: "It's a joke to run a marathon by walking every other mile or by finishing in six, seven, eight hours. It used to be that running a marathon was worth something—there used to be a pride saying that you ran a marathon, but not anymore. Now it's, 'How low is the bar?' "

Maybe the bar is low; but so, too, are the blows. The judgments strangers put on my marathon time—or my 5K time or my sprint-triathlon time or how much I bench press—can play to my own self-doubts. The low blow hurts because it confirms the worst suspicions I have about myself—that I'm a fraud and not worthy of claiming the identity of runner, marathoner, or athlete.

It can be easy to fixate on one negative comment rather than a whole slew of positive ones. Ironman World Champion Chrissy Wellington would routinely return to the finish line hours after her victory to hand out medals to those back-of-the-pack-ers, the ones just hoping to cross the line in time to be official finishers. Many elite endurance athletes return to the finish line to celebrate the slowest athletes. This simple action helps to validate those back-of-the-pack-ers. They realize their winning time is not degraded by the pace of the last-place finisher.

Everyone traveled over the same course.

Everyone faced the same conditions.

Everyone suffered physically.

Everyone had to face doubt at some point.

It's just that some did it faster than others.

We are all out there, singing our own woeful country tune of misery and heartache. We are all looking for redemption at the finish line, a capstone to a journey that showed us hope and joy while facing the depths of our fears and personal demons.

So what about those critics who lament the degradation of the solemnity of the marathon? Perhaps the best response I heard came from an episode of the podcast Magic Lessons with writer Elizabeth Gilbert (Episdoe 208: "Leap Into the Fire"). Her guest, fellow writer Martha Beck, said her response to critics was often: "I respectfully do not care."

It's an attitude easier for me to invoke in hindsight, emotionally removed from the sting of condescending critique (the most unhelpful form of critique) and the disdainful disapproval of my slowness. But as I cultivate that attitude, the voice of my inner athlete becomes easier to hear. Pace is for our amusement, she tells me. It's something to keep us occupied and to mix up our training. At her best, my inner athlete uses pace to push me out of my comfort zone. So you think you can't run that fast, eh? my inner athlete says. Why are you setting limits on yourself without trying first?

Good question.

I've had prolonged text-message conversations with my friend Nate (himself being a two-time Boston Marathon qualifier) on the eve of my races. We'd discuss pace and my race plan, almost always a slight variation on the same theme: start slow, finish fast. But Nate would challenge me from time to time, especially if I was running a 5K.

"Why not just go all-out from the start and see what happens?" Nate asked me. "What's the worst that can happen?"

"I'd blow up," I responded. My fear was that by going out too fast in a 5K I wouldn't be able to hold the pace and would fall apart by the halfway point, or sooner. The end result would be a pretty crappy 5K time.

But Nate challenged me further.

"So you blow up," he said. "So what? People get too precious about their times. I say just go for it."

What if I *did* just go for it? What if I went out super hard and blew up in the middle of the race and had to jog the rest of the course? Did I fail to be an athlete because I decided to test my limits that day? Were the final results always a measure of my worth as an athlete? Was I only an athlete when I was working for a very specific, measurable goal, like running a sub-two-hour half-marathon? Was my worth as an athlete only based on if I accomplished those goals?

Again, my inner athlete was screaming "LISTEN TO ME!"

And when I fell back into old patterns of doubting myself, I found another perspective-check in a conversation with world champion mountain-biker Rebecca Rusch. She also had to deal with the deflating edge of sharp criticism. Only not because she was the back of the back.

She was sharply criticized for *winning*.

Defying Odds, Overcoming Obstacles

It was 2006 and Rebecca Rusch had just won her first national title, taking the USA Cycling 24-Hour Mountain Bike National Championship. She then came in second at the world championships. Not bad for a newbie to the sport after a career as a rock climber and adventure racer. She was winning at the highest levels of mountain biking . . . but not everyone celebrated her story.

She overheard the conversations on the course.

"There's this girl out there who is so stiff and uncoordinated, it's actually painful to watch," Rebecca recalled in her book *Rush to Glory: Adventure, Risk & Triumph on the Path Less Traveled*. "I can tell this girl is not a cyclist. Who is she? What is she even doing here?"

Then came the bigger blow when a mountain-biking magazine wrote a feature story on Rebecca. The headline? "Winning Ugly."

It wasn't just the "winning ugly" part which served up a gut-wrenching blow to Rebecca. It was downplaying her accomplishments, because her style didn't fit the technical mold of an elite bike racer.

She would get off her bike and walk around and over difficult obstacles. She knew she was a gear masher. She knew she was learning technique both in racing and in training. But just because she wasn't yet technically proficient didn't mean she couldn't find a way through.

Always gracious with her time to encourage others through her own life story, Rebecca spoke with me about the blow to her self-esteem and how she moved past it.

"The article basically said how is this girl who is a terrible bike rider winning races?" Rebecca recalled. "And it really hurt me when I read that at the time. I started cycling late. My technique wasn't very good. I'd jump off and on over hard spots and jump back on my bike but kept going. That hurt my feelings at the time—Look how crappy of a bike rider she is. My ego was embarrassed. I was a pro rider but a shitty bike rider.

"Now when I look back, I'm proud of that. I sucked but I still won races. I was still good enough to win races and that launched a whole other career for me of riding bikes. If I had listened to that article that said I sucked, that I was a terrible bike rider, I don't know what job I would have now. It would have been sad because I would have missed out on this opportunity."

So hold the phone for a moment. Rebecca Rusch was winning races. *National championship* races. She was finishing among the best in the world in endurance mountain-bike race events. And she had to deal with criticism—the kind which cuts to your core because it challenges your perception of yourself, disregards your accomplishments, and scoffs at your dreams—all because her technique was unconventional. She didn't look like the other bike racers, so she must not be a bike racer.

If a woman who earned the nickname "Queen of Pain" while traveling the world climbing, running, kayaking, and biking had times where she was bothered by doubts about her place as an athlete, well . . . no wonder a back-of-the-pack-er like me also struggled. In a way, her story gave me hope. Other women—*world champions*, even—also had to win their personal battles with doubt, with ill-placed feelings of inferiority.

Success does not make you immune from doubt.

Mountain biking is Rebecca's second athletic career. Born in 1968 on the cusp of Title IX, she grew up in suburban Chicago with some of her earliest memories of camping, playing in the dirt, and doing tomboy sorts of things.

She followed her passion for outdoor sports and climbing to California and discovered adventure racing, becoming a participant and team captain for *Eco-Challenge: The Expedition Race*, created by TV producer Mark Burnett and largely considered to be the genesis for reality television. She went all over the world, navigating remote and treacherous trails by hiking, climbing, rafting, cycling—all while trying to beat other teams.

But soon, the professional adventure-racing series came to an end and Rebecca needed to find a new gig. She told her sponsors, and Red Bull decided that since she had a year left on her sponsorship contract, they would continue to pay her.

"All my other sponsors left and Red Bull came to me and said, 'You have a year left on your contract, just find something cool to do,'" Rebecca recalled.

That's how she came to mountain-bike racing. She started that career with those "ugly wins" before winning over the critics with her domination of grueling events. She won the Leadville Trail 100 MTB four times. She won the 24 Hour Solo Mountain Bike World Championships three times.

Through the events and her championships, she began talking with more women. From professional riders to recreational cyclists who rode on weekends, all expressed the same theme to her over and over again: perfectionism was holding so many people back. She would hold group rides for women of all levels and notice their feeling of failure when they had to get off their bikes and walk up a hill or around a difficult obstacle.

They didn't do it perfectly. They didn't do it like everyone else.

Therefore, they felt like failures.

But Rebecca knows about not doing things like everyone else. She moved past her feeling of embarrassment of "winning ugly" to preach a new ethic, one that favors the process of moving forward regardless of how it looks to outsiders.

"If we just try, it might not look pretty, but if you try often times that's enough," Rebecca said. "I'm not saying we shouldn't put our best foot forward but we hold ourselves back wanting everything to be perfect. It's never the right time for me to do this. That's why you encourage people to try. If you walk down a hill you can't do, that's fine. You didn't turn away and go backward."

Finding My Way Up the Mountain

Mountain biking was proving not to be my thing. I was in the beginner group in Winter Park, Colorado on my retreat with Women's Quest. The first day of mountain biking was about learning the basics.

And I mean *the basics*. I had been training for this adventure by riding my grandmother's old Tyler, complete with coaster brakes and two speeds—*go* and *stop*. I had never been on a mountain bike before and the closest thing to riding "off road" would be hitting a patch of gravel on the shoulder of a paved road and going into a panic that I would crash.

Shifting was new to me. Even when I rode a 10-speed around my neighborhood as a kid I never quite understood the gears. Then again, I was riding in a flat residential area on smoothly paved roads. I only needed to be able to pedal at a comfortable rate. No need to touch the gears. So there was no deeply buried knowledge I could unearth on the dirt trails, nothing technical to come back to me.

Our instructor that day was fantastic and patient. She took us through the gears. She showed us how to ride over small branches and rocks. I struggled at the back of the beginners group, uncertain about the difference between "gear up" and "gear down." Is *up* closer to the bike frame? Or away? Am I moving both sets of gears? Or just one? And which shifter moves which set of gears again? I didn't quite get it, but I was learning.

Then came the next day.

There was a small group of women who were driven to the trails at the top of a mountain. They were injured—and then there was June, who was seventy-six years old—and so they got a ride to the top. How I wished I had a ride to the top. Two of the women turned back as we struggled up this mountain (which probably was more of a hill, but to me, and to a few of us, this was mountain rising out of the great Colorado range, formidable and impassable). Moments after they left, I wished I had gone with them. Why didn't I turn back, too? Why couldn't I have gotten a ride to the top? The steepness of the trail was something I'd never experienced on a bike before. Forget trying to change my gears; I was trying not to fall backward and off the bike. I was fighting back tears. I couldn't turn the pedals over. There was still quite a ways to go up to the top. I got off my bike and announced I was going to go back.

A chorus of "No!" replied. I had come so far, the chorus said. Don't stop now!

Then Barb came up to me. "I'll walk up with you," she said.

I shook my head. She could ride up the mountain. I didn't want to hold her back and ruin her experience. She deserved the triumph of riding to the top.

"No, really, I'll walk with you," Barb said. She had injured her hamstring on a group run the first day. She was struggling a bit, too. I wasn't holding her back. In fact, walking up was probably the prudent thing for her to do to still enjoy the biking while not further aggravating her hamstring.

I wiped the tears on the back of my glove and agreed.

We pushed our bikes up to the top of the hill, which was slightly easier than riding them, but slow and arduous. Once at the top, I found beautifully wooded trails lined softly with old pine needles and a crisp air. I rode at the back of a small group, with two staff members making sure I didn't get lost as I dropped contact with the main group. It wasn't so much about being slow as it was breathing in the experience—the sights, the sounds, the feel. I was riding my bike in a postcard and I wanted to seal the memory in my mind.

I fell once on the descent as we made our way as a group back to the parking lot. A bunch of women fell at the same spot. Muddy and dusty but uninjured, I encountered a new problem—how to get back on the bike. I fell because it was a steep and gravely part of the downhill trail. If I got on at that point, I was sure to fall off or start flying down the hill and hit that tree in front of me. *What do I do? Walk my bike down?*

I walked over a bit, away from the gravel, managed to get back on my bike, and started feathering the brakes immediately. (If there was one thing I remember from this mountain-biking venture it was feathering the brakes.)

I made it back down the mountain in one piece. Back at the lodge, the two women who turned back came running up to me. They hugged me. "You did it! I'm so happy for you!"

It wasn't pretty. It wasn't textbook. My shorts were caked in mud and my legs were cut up with scratches from thorny forest growth.

But I did it.

A feeling of accomplishment rose through my body. I was elated. I was tired and sore but smiling. I was so happy that I didn't bail and walk back to town. It was perhaps my first true encounter with my own strength, my own perseverance. I had been full of doubt, ready to turn back. I had been embarrassed by my inability to ride my bike up the hill. I'd bought into a story I'd told myself somewhere along the way that I was weak and meek and not suited for great adventures.

But on that bike, amongst a group of supportive women who believed anything was possible, I made one decision—to keep going forward. That was all I had to do. I didn't have to mash gears or grind out the hill or whiz past others while jumping tree roots. All I had to do was keep moving forward.

It sounds easy, but some days it's the most difficult thing to do.

Ironman on the Horizon

It was New Year's Day and we were watching a new tradition on one of the cable stations: a TV marathon of NBC's Ironman World Championships coverage. I was with a group of my new triathlon friends. I had been contemplating doing an Ironman myself, or more specifically an Iron Distance race. (Ironman has been trademarked by the World Triathlon Corporation, but other companies put on triathlons of the same distance: 2.4-mile swim, 112-mile bike ride, 26.2-mile run. To avoid trademark infringement, they are called "Iron Distance" events.)

I was full of doubt about this particular journey. I had just learned to swim three years ago, and while I was still among the last swimmers out of the water, I had found a comfortable—albeit non-traditional—rhythm to my swim. My cycling was at its best and my run had improved. There was no reason for me *not* to dive into an Ironman.

With one exception.

My fear.

What if I couldn't finish the swim before the cutoff? That was my biggest obstacle. I'd also never ridden a hundred miles on my bike, and I only had the one marathon under my belt. This was a big undertaking. Very big. Who was I to think I could do it?

I gave voice to my fears while talking to the coach that afternoon as we watched the coverage of old Ironman World Championships in Hawaii. Among the professionals and the elite age-group qualifiers were stories that tugged at your heart strings. They were emotional stories about personal loss. People had worked through the deaths of loved ones and overcome illness and injury to toe the starting line in Hawaii.

In the definition of "athlete" put forth by the sport ethic, these were the people who were defying odds and overcoming obstacles. Not me. I had (knock on wood) no serious injuries or illnesses. The death of my grandmother certainly shook my world, but people lose someone they love every day.

The only obstacle in the way was me.

And while that might not be what normally comes to mind when we think of athletes as people who defy odds and overcome obstacles, our own insecurities can be the most difficult challenge to move beyond.

Being Mean to Myself

By 2014, Rebecca was doing fewer elite races and more connecting. She'd created a bicycling event, "Rebecca's Private Idaho," to not only showcase the underestimated landscape of her adopted hometown of Ketchem, Idaho, but to encourage girls and women from all backgrounds to be active. She advocates (and so do I!) for all women to call themselves athletes as a way to widen our identities.

"It's funny how we put ourselves in boxes," Rebecca said. "A lot of women I ride with, they don't consider themselves an athlete because they're not professional or not doing races or not winning anything. The definition of an athlete doesn't just mean that. I try to encourage women to say 'I am an athlete.'

"We're terribly mean to ourselves. We hold ourselves back with lack of confidence and negative talk to ourselves. Time after time, it comes up when I think I can't do something. You take a bike ride and in the end when you do it with friends, they're helping you muster up the courage to do it. That feeling then of looking back and going, 'Oh my gosh, I did that! I rode that hill!' It's a pretty addictive feeling of achievement. I thought I couldn't do it and then I did it.

"It's a lesson I have to learn a million times over again."

So I'm not the only one who likes to beat herself up for her perceived misgivings.

I'm not the only one with a tendency to qualify what I've done and what I've accomplished with the phrase, "Yeah, but . . ."

Because that's what I do. Over and over again. Especially when it comes to athletic pursuits.

You're a runner? Yeah, but I'm slow.

You're a triathlete? Yeah, but I'm a terrible swimmer.

You've done an Ironman? Yeah, but only one race.

Yeah, I train, but not as hard as other people. And I don't particularly like the way I look in a triathlon suit. And photos of me running almost always look as if they should carry the subtitle "How *Not* to Run." Like a before-and-after photo, and I was the *before*.

But there are instances, glorious spaces of time, when I'm not all up in my head. Times when I'm in the moment, when I'm feeling my body, when I'm not thinking of where my particular performance ranks on the great imaginary athletic scale. When I've finished a tough workout or crossed a finish line. Often, it comes when I've put the watch away. Instead of timing myself in order to *judge* myself, I've just gone out—for a long hike, or to run challenging hills, or to ride my bike for as long as I can hold out.

In those moments, I feel accomplished.

In those moments, I say to myself, "Look at what you just did!"

When I stop being mean to myself—when I stop judging myself—the athlete inside of me can just play. She can be joyful. She can try new things, push through limitations, and accept when that's the best effort she had for the day. When I let go of the negative self-talk (for which I could have a gold medal, if negative self-talk were an Olympic sport), the only things left are possibility, wonder, and joy.

To let go of that negative self-talk to allow myself to try, regardless of the outcome, is a lesson I'm constantly relearning as well.

Chapter 6: Comparison Is the Thief of Joy

You Can't Judge a Runner at the Start Line

It was a hot July morning and the runners were roaming around the start line.

I wasn't part of this 10K. I came to meet my friend, who was volunteering with the setup. We were going to watch the runners take off, then go have breakfast.

It was my second year of triathlon and my focus was on my first 70.3-mile race in the fall. I'd met a wide variety of people in the running community, many also newbies and novices who followed my athletic chronicles on my blog. That's how I met Elizabeth, a woman who was about my age and a year or two into her own athletic-running foray. We'd emailed a few times and chatted at races, not really friends but more acquaintances.

She spotted me at the start line and came rushing over.

"I beat you!" she said, never bothering to say hello.

Um, I'm sorry?

"I beat you!" she said again, her smile so big I thought it would leap off her face while she clearly restrained her body from doing a victory dance. "I looked up your last 5K time and I can't believe it but I beat you!" She was gleeful. Positively gleeful.

Well, good for you?

I smiled and nodded and mumbled some type of congratulations.

It wasn't that I was upset that she beat me.

It's just that I didn't even realize we were competing.

For any snarky readers out there, yes, I know it's a race. The goal is to finish ahead of as many people as you can, preferably in your gender's age group. Part of the athlete identity is competition. And competition means people are divided into winners and losers.

Clearly this woman, whom I barely knew, wanted to win over me. Like, really wanted to beat me. Very badly.

I didn't have that same drive.

My approach to racing was to see what I could do, not necessarily what I could do in relation to other people. I was in competition with *myself*. I wanted to set a personal record in every race, to best my last race. My competition essentially became the clock. But there was another approach to competition, one which had me dueling it out with my own negative thoughts. I wasn't battling other runners as much as I was battling fear and doubt in my head—the voices which encouraged me to live small and keep expectations low so I didn't hurt myself, physically or emotionally. I was in the race to see what I could do for me.

But even with the best of intentions, it was easy to get sucked into comparing myself to other runners.

It started with my first few road races. I'd get to the start line and look around at the other runners, trying to decipher who would be fast and who would be slow. I'd think, *Try to stay with this person,* or *I should totally beat that person.*

I learned quickly that you truly can't judge a runner at the start line. That person who looks a bit heavy and is wearing workout gear from Target? She will smoke you. That person who looks like she stepped off the cover of a running magazine? You'll pass her in the first mile.

Later on, I learned how to use other runners as motivation. Sometimes it was the halfway point, when I was starting to fade. *See that woman in the green hoody? Stay up with her. Don't let her get too far ahead. That guy in the Michigan T-shirt? He's running about your pace. Tuck in behind him and pace off him.*

Once the finish line was in view, I'd dial it in. I'd try to catch that woman in the green hoody before the line. Sometimes I did. Sometimes I didn't. After the race I'd often try to find the person who pulled me along, who kept me working hard because I was trying to stay up with them or catch them. I'd thank them. Even if they beat me, I thanked them. Because they helped bring out the best in me that day.

Competition turned into comparison rather quickly for me. The triathlon coach I was working with told me the first year would be about *experience*, the second year about *performance*. So part of my first year of gaining experience was watching how other runners and triathletes went about their training and racing. And this easily flowed into comparing myself to them. Comparing how dedicated I was to my training. Comparing how I ate and how I tracked my nutrition.

Comparing my results.

The inner competition which brought out the best in me devolved outward into constant comparison to other athletes. And I was always coming up short in my analysis.

The saying "Comparison is the thief of joy" is most often attributed to Teddy Roosevelt and its timelessness as a cliché remains because it rings so true. The more I compared myself to what other runners around me were doing—particularly when it came to results—my joy in running and racing diminished.

Running with Friends

It's night and I'm alone in my apartment thinking about my most recent morning run. I'm reliving the struggle to keep up with my dear friend on what was supposed to be an "easy" run. But it wasn't easy for me. And now I'm full of doubts and tears.

My friend told me she was going to be slow. A "toad"—that's what she had called herself. But after the first mile she started to slowly pull ahead of me, chatting with others in the group. It didn't take long for my friend and this so-called slow easy-paced group to become dots in the distance.

I was sad and mad at the same time. Frustration boiled that I couldn't keep up with their simple, slow pace. Why were they just easily jogging along, having full conversations and laughing, and I was winded and struggling and half a mile behind? Anger toward my friend seeped in there, too, because despite her "toad" pace she'd ditched me.

At least that's how it felt. She didn't really ditch me. About every mile or so she would circle back to me, to make sure I was doing OK. I fought the tears but muttered an apology. "I suck. I'm sorry," I said.

"Pace is just for our amusement," she came back with. "You don't suck."

But I felt I did. My good-ol' sidekick, fear, was present, with plenty of I-told-you-sos about being an athlete or a runner. *You can't even keep up with your friend! She admits to running a toad's pace, yet you're so bad she has to stop running and backtrack to check on you!* I sulked the rest of the run and through our breakfast afterward.

By nighttime, I was feeling sorry for the sulking and sent her a text apologizing.

That's two apologies in one day. First for being slow. Then for sulking about being slow.

She responded with kindness, as she always did. Then went on her own personal self-denigration campaign. She said how slow she had become since undergoing chemotherapy for breast cancer a few years ago. She used to be much faster.

As a side note, I knew she had achieved the honor of being named an All-American in track during her time in junior college. While she was in forties. She never talked about this and only meekly answered questions when you asked her about it. I would have been waving that shit around like an overweight middle-age man who still tells with crystal-clear detail the story of how he hit a game-winning shot in a high-school basketball game.

Not my friend.

After debating which one of us was slowest and hence the worse runner, our text conversation devolved into discussions of weight. I would usually start it by saying I was fat and slow. She would tell me I wasn't fat (and, by the way, not that slow). She told me I was beautiful and strong and that I was perfect just the way I was. Her words would have held more credibility, would have been a true shot of confidence, if it wasn't for her putting herself down in the process. She complained about her own weight and the look of her body as well. And I didn't understand it. She was a hundred pounds—if that—soaking wet, and fit and trim. She was smart and funny and a good runner.

If she thought *she* was slow and fat, what chance in hell did *I* have?

We had these conversations often. On the one hand, it made me feel less alone. I wasn't the only person who thought she was slow and fat and frustrated by this notion that her outward appearance and results weren't matching what she really felt on the inside.

But on the other hand, the conversations could be demoralizing. Was anyone ever happy with who they were in the moment? Were we all living for that "someday"—that day when you lose twenty pounds, when you can run an eight-minute mile, when you have money in your savings account?

In my eyes, my friend had it all when it came to being a runner. She was faster than me and could be consistent. She was smaller but powerful, quiet with a force and able to keep a perspective when things went bad. She tried so hard to build me up, but for the most part the words she used to celebrate my accomplishments rang hollow in my ears. She said great things about me—how strong I was, how solid my running had become, how impressed she was with my cycling, how good I looked.

But she was so hard on herself.

How could I believe the things she said about me if she didn't believe those wonderful things about herself?

Even Lindsey Vonn Doesn't Have It Figured Out

It was a non-descript day in October when I was driving to work, listening to my local NPR station as I often do. That's when the program *On Point* caught my attention with its upcoming guest, world-champion skier Lindsey Vonn. The program, which aired on October 20, 2016 from WBUR in Boston, focused on Vonn's new book, *Strong is the New*

Beautiful: Embrace Your Natural Beauty, Eat Clean, and Harness Your Power. Vonn's media-publicity tour championed the notion that all women, regardless of size, are beautiful. The power lies in our perception and belief about ourselves.

The introduction piqued my curiosity. Then Lindsey dropped this truth-bomb:

"I've always been pretty insecure and I feel like I've always been different than other people. I'm bigger. I'm more muscular. As my friends used to say, I'm big-boned, and I've never really been 100 percent confident in myself. I'm very, very confident, probably the most confident person you'll ever find on the mountain. But off the mountain, I am very insecure and just, I don't know, I've never really felt beautiful enough."

Hold the phone.

Lindsey Vonn has never felt beautiful enough. The American cover girl for the Winter Olympics has never felt secure about her looks. I mean, if Lindsey Vonn struggled with body-image insecurity then no wonder the rest of us mere mortals get sucked into the "not good enough" void.

The program's host politely challenged her, asking the same question I had while listening in my Subaru Outback.

"Really?"

"Yes, really," Lindsey said. It may have started as a kid, a time she said she never fit in—partly from traveling and partly from rocking the braces, bangs, and perm look. She outgrew the awkward years and in 2010 found herself on top of the world winning Olympic gold. That launched her into popular culture, and while on that circuit she started down the dangerous road of comparison.

"I was kind of thrown into red-carpet situations and being around actresses and models and beautiful people," Lindsey said. "I just didn't feel like I fit in. I felt like I didn't belong and I wasn't really happy with the way I looked and it made me question my weight, and do I need to look a certain way to be in these situations, and it took a little bit of hit on my skiing."

She'd put an emphasis on diet and exercise toward how she looked compared to these actresses and models instead of fueling her skiing. Her confident comfort zone crumbled in 2011 when, after winning three straight World Cup titles, she lost to Germany's Maria Riesch.

"I started to watch what I ate more and tried different diets," Lindsey said of her post-2010 Olympic tour. "I ended up losing the World Cup overall title by three points that season. I think that had a large part to do with being insecure and not just accepting what I am and training as hard as I can to be strong, instead of trying to be skinny and fit into this image that I thought I need to fit into."

Put her on skis on the top of a mountain and she believes she will conquer the world. Put her among some entertainment celebrities after winning the Olympic gold medal in 2010 and she spirals into self-doubt. Then again, who wouldn't?

"What you think looks normal on TV is not in reality, it's so much thinner and smaller than you think it would be," Lindsey said. "So when I was actually next to these people, I was thinking, 'Wow. I am out of my league. I am three times the size of these human beings.'"

She changed her attitude from *seeking skinny* to *building strong*. In 2012 she captured her fourth overall World Cup title, becoming just the second woman to win that many titles, while in 2016 she won her twentieth World Cup crystal-globe title—the most by any skier, male or female.

And along the way she's changed the way she sees her body.

"My body has gotten me to this point—to win the Olympics, to win more World Cups than any woman in history, and I'm proud of that," Lindsey said.

Lindsey keeps talking about it, keeps talking about *strong* being *beautiful*, because as she toured the country to promote her book she met hundreds of girls who were still struggling with similar issues—with having an "athletic" body-type, not looking like their friends and feeling left out.

" 'Strong is beautiful' is not a new concept, but it is still something that a lot of people struggle with," Lindsey said. "It's one thing to say that strong is beautiful and that we accept that as a society. It's another thing to actually feel that."

Even world-class skiers with Olympic gold medals struggle to feel that sometimes.

So imagine what their *friends* feel like.

Learning to Wear the Dunce Cap

Report cards came out four times a year. In elementary school they weren't really grades; we were given notations for *Superior, Satisfactory, Needs Improvement,* and *Unsatisfactory.* The majority of my marks were *Superior* because, well, I loved school, and I also loved to please people in authority.

When Sunday rolled around, I took my report card to show Gram. I'm not sure "proud" was the right word to describe how I felt about my report card. I felt good grades were expected. Of *course* I would get good grades. Not because I was exceedingly smart or entitled but because I loved to learn. No, really. I was the girl who would ace the test and still ask for extra credit.

Still, I showed Gram my report card with a big smile and immense happiness and a sense that I had done what was asked of me. Gram would look it over, smile, and praise me for my grades.

Then everything shifted. Gram was still smiling, her tone jovial but her words jarring.

"You just want to keep me in the corner, don't you?" Gram said. "I'm just sitting in the corner wearing a dunce cap. Gram is just a big dunce. You're keeping me the dunce."

No! Gram, you're not a dunce! Why would you say that? I don't want you to sit in the corner and wear a dunce cap!

While sarcasm was readily spoken in my family, her joking about being a dunce never felt very funny. Probably because she was displaying a deep-seated belief about herself, one that had been reinforced by society and deeply internalized.

One that I disagreed with.

At the time I didn't know the backstory. I didn't know that Gram never graduated from high school, leaving a month early to take a job so that the family could send her oldest sister to nursing school. I didn't know that she basically flunked out of Polish school, unable to read past a third-grade level in the language of her family. And those were just the stories I learned about when I was older; there are surely other ones which reinforced my grandmother's version of herself as the dunce.

As a child I didn't know any of that. Nor did I really care. Gram was awesome. She sang songs with me and told great stories, lots of stories. She showered me with love—which usually took the form of food and gifts. On sleepovers at her house she would bring me breakfast in bed. I mean, how cool is that? I loved her. She loved me. That should have been the end of the story.

But she didn't seem to be at peace with herself. She called herself a dunce. She called herself fat. And I was listening. The message was passed down. I received and internalized the message without thinking. It was the cue I was given. My reflex became to downplay my accomplishments. I didn't want someone I loved (like my grandmother) to feel bad about themselves because I had done something—whether it be good grades, an award, or a marathon finish. And anyway, women weren't supposed to brag about themselves. They were supposed to point out their own flaws before anyone else had the chance to.

But there was hope for me.

My longing to be an athlete drew me into new adventures and outside my comfort zone. That desire became more powerful than those childhood messages of fear and living small in order to protect myself from physical harm and emotional vulnerability. That desire led me to opportunities to practice bravery.

As an adult, I learned bits and pieces about what a truly colorful life my grandmother lived. I wish I could go back and ask her about it, demand that she tell me more stories while being vigilant about documenting the details so they weren't lost to the unreliability of my memory. But I can't. Instead, I decided to honor her by doing what she couldn't, or at least what she couldn't in my eyes. I would go outside my comfort zone, physically speaking—run races and learn to swim and do other hard things I never thought I could will my body to do. I would go outside my comfort zone, emotionally speaking—challenge myself to listen to my own heart and learn from the mistakes of following the crowd.

These new adventures (which she would most definitely describe as "nuts") are memorialized by the collection of finisher's medals which adorn my living room walls. I've had to move past the naysayers who believe I'm bragging about my accomplishments—the people who say you shouldn't do races for the medals, that it's just more "stuff."

But my finisher's medals tell a tale. I can pick up each one and tell you a story about the race—about the conditions, the course, my training, the city, the people around me on the journey. They are evidence of my bravery. They are evidence that I can do hard things. Evidence that I can change my own mentality, adjust my approach, move from experience to results and back to experience again.

They tell the story of my journey with my athletic self.

Chapter 7: Misadventures In the Wild

Finding Belva Lockwood

I'm not sure which I remember first—the library or the ravine.

Both were enchanting places of my childhood. The library was a big, beautiful old stone building, nestled among other big old buildings on Main Street in Lockport. The large Roman columns and the creamy-gray stone spoke of importance and earnestness to my five-year-old self. The children's room was in the basement with its own entrance, down the steps to the right of the gigantic heavy red door. The only gravitas in this room were the books themselves, the stacks and stacks of books that I couldn't wait to read.

I would head upstairs to the adult library—the "real" library, as I thought of it—and sit at one of the massive mahogany tables to start reading while my mom went through the stacks with her list of books she wanted to read clutched in her hand. Usually she came away disappointed, but always with her own stack of books.

They were so thick! I didn't know how she read them all from start to finish. Truth be told, I sometimes didn't finish my own books. I especially struggled to get through Laura Ingalls Wilder's *Little House on the Prairie* series, in part because it was just easier to watch the series on television. Julie Campbell Tatham's books about Trixie Belden, with her tomboy ways and gang of ragtag friends who went off solving mysteries, on the other hand—*those* I finished. Each and every one.

The adventures of Trixie Belden sparked my imagination when I went to my other sacred childhood place: the Royalton Ravine.

This was the first time I ever remember hiking. The library was a space for me and Mom; the ravine was a space for me and Dad. Royalton Ravine was magical because it had the swinging bridge—the long, fun, and sometimes fear-inducing swinging bridge. The wood-planked suspension bridge runs across Eighteen Mile Creek and it was always the highlight of this particular walk in the woods. I called it "hiking," but Dad called it "going for a walk."

"Time in the woods is always time well spent," my dad said once, leaving a lasting impression on my mind.

At the library, my mother introduced me to the power of storytelling. Words became a way for me to make sense of the world. At the little Niagara County park, my father introduced me to the love of the outdoors, to the freedom and joy of movement. If words were the way I made sense of the world, running through the woods was the way I entered into communion with the world.

As a little kid, the park was huge and the trail was long. Revisiting it as an adult, I discovered the trail from end to end is only about a mile, with a short but steep descent into the ravine and a short but steep climb out. There's a small waterfall (which apparently paled in comparison to the bridge in my childhood because I have few memories of its existence), along with ruins of a house from the late 1800s. Years later I discovered they are believed to be the remains of the home where Belva Lockwood was born, the first woman officially recognized as running for President of the United States (in 1884 and 1888) and the first woman ever admitted to practice law before the Supreme Court.

Turns out I had spent wonderful summer days of my childhood romping around Belva Lockwood's childhood home, although her story had been lost in the footnotes of history. There was something tragic about the forgotten story of Belva Lockwood. It was as if Belva had an asterisk next to her name, like the ones that appear in sports almanacs next to former great players, qualifying their record-setting performances for posterity because of real (or perceived) transgressions against the game.

I never learned about her in school despite the fact I grew up a stone's throw from her birthplace (and spent my entire elementary-school education learning local history through the Erie Canal song).

It wasn't until I hit forty that I finally found a well-researched biography of Belva (*Belva Lockwood: The Woman Who Would Be President*, NYU Press, 2007), discovering she fell out of favor with the powerful women suffragists of the day with a penchant for self-promotion and a platform of radical peace. Her twenty-first-century biographer Jill Norgren wrote that Belva's slide into obscurity happened because, at the time of her death in 1917, few libraries collected the papers of women activists. In addition, after falling on hard financial times Belva had to move into a small apartment before her death, and her collection of papers and books were left to family members who then decluttered their space by sending most of them off to donation sites and paper mills.

I walked into the Royalton Ravine, down the steep slope, and across the wooden suspension bridge that didn't seem as long as when I was a child but certainly held on to its element of adventure with its swing and occasional missing board. I climbed up the other side of the creek and stood among what remained of Belva Lockwood's childhood home. The brick ruins are now covered in typical teenage graffiti, overgrown and largely forgotten—not unlike the story of her life's work.

There's an odd connection here. Between me and Belva. Between me and the ravine.

Her story was forgotten, obscured by circumstance and paved over by time. But it had been recovered, at least partially. Her place in history had been revived, although her impact on history never truly disappeared. Her work for women's suffrage, for women's legal and financial rights, for building peace—all that had an impact on the world she lived in, all of it influenced history in subtle but meaningful ways.

Thinking about Belva in this ravine, a place filled with my own personal history, my mind wandered to my inner athlete.

In this space, on walks with my dad at six years old, is where I first met my inner athlete.

In the exuberance of training for my first triathlon to the disappointment of missing my goals in a half-marathon, I had forgotten this original meeting with my inner athlete. For as long as I can remember I went for hikes, as a child with my dad and later trekking on well-marked trails alone as an adult. There was freedom and discovery and a sense of being on the trail that I could not experience any place else.

How had I missed this?

Just as Belva's story was forgotten at Royalton Ravine, so too, it seemed, had my own story of my athletic origins disappeared somewhere in these woods.

The Joy of the Trail

I always hiked with Dad. It's just what we did. From the first forays at Royalton Ravine on the swinging bridge to walks at Iroquois Wildlife Refuge or Bond Lake, we always spent time on trails. Usually they were easy walks. On occasion we tackled challenging trails at Allegany State Park, on the edge of the Allegheny mountains on New York's border with Pennsylvania.

Once we thought we were extraordinarily clever. I was in my early twenties, fresh out of college and living about half an hour away from Allegany State Park, when we planned to do a six-mile trail. It was the longest hike we'd ever attempted with a park-rating of "difficult." We saw on the trail map that the start- and end-points were not the same, so we decided to take two cars and park one at the trailhead and one at the finish.

And off we went.

As self-taught hikers at the dawn of the mass-Internet age, we didn't have much information other than the length of the trail and the very basic park map. We were short-day hikers, not backpackers, and so didn't bring enough really important things.

Like, oh, you know, food and water.

We had only a general idea of the terrain we'd be facing. So for us, the 700-foot climb in the first 3.5 miles was excruciatingly difficult. We huffed and puffed and stopped to catch our breath with the hope that our legs would stop feeling like they were rubber on fire. We figured we had to be at the top of the ridge . . . but suddenly we were climbing again.

We hugged trees for dear life. We forged a stream (well, crossed a small shallow one, anyway) and with delirious delight emerged at the end of the trail. We were exhausted and spent but felt accomplished. The challenge was accepted and completed.

Now all I could think about was food. Lots and lots of food.

There, just where we'd parked it, was my car. Only as we walked over to it did I realize the tragic truth: I had left my car keys in my dad's car back at the trailhead. A wave of panic swept over me. *I can't go back on that trail,* I thought. *I can't hike those six miles back. That's just crazy.*

Too. Much. Pain. Need. Water.

"I bet we can just walk along the road," my dad said. And sure enough, it was a short walk back to my dad's car. He unlocked it and sat down, grateful for the rest. I frantically pulled up the floor mat on the passenger side and there they were—my car keys. Safe and sound. Though our great master plan for the hike was foiled.

We drove into Olean to eat at Ponderosa because they were all about massive buffets going all the time . . . and we were all about immediacy of food, not quality of food.

This botched hike became our ongoing joke and was my first inkling of a life lesson I'd discover more fully later on, and that I'd like to share with you now.

The best stories often come from mistakes and perceived failures.

I loved hiking, both with my dad and by myself. We explored the outdoors as curious, albeit often uninformed, participants. It had never occurred to me this type of activity was athletic, never occurred to me this might qualify me as an athlete. I felt like I was just walking in the woods.

I wasn't training. I wasn't racing. I wasn't part of a group or team.

There was no purpose, no goal, no competition.

There wasn't anything extraordinary to it—just put on good-soled shoes and follow the marked trail. Surely there had to be something more to being an athlete, right? Surely what I was doing didn't qualify me as an athlete or athletic. I was merely someone who enjoyed hiking.

But the more time I spent on trails, the more I wanted to do. That meant putting myself in a situation where I could embrace an adventure— where I was healthy and strong and fit enough to tackle hiking up a steep hill or riding my bike a long distance, healthy and strong and fit enough to hold my own on a whitewater-rafting trip.

What if my love of hiking meant I was already an athlete?

But . . . could I call myself an athlete just because of that?

Once again, I discovered that uncertainty in claiming an athletic identity was not unique to me.

Results Over Experience

Heather "Anish" Anderson has a knack for traveling long distances in the backcountry. Quickly. By herself. Anish has done six hundred-mile ultramarathons, but her claim to fame is setting the record for the fastest known time on a self-supported thru-hike through three of the major trails in the United States—the 2,650-mile Pacific Crest Trail (sixty days, seventeen hours, twelve minutes in 2013), the 2,200-mile Appalachian Trail (fifty-four days, seven hours, forty-eight minutes in 2015) and the 800-mile Arizona Trail (nineteen days, seventeen hours, nine minutes in 2016).

She has hiked more than 19,000 backcountry miles, and while she sees herself as an athlete, she doesn't necessarily call herself that in public.

"I feel the general perception when you say you're an athlete is that you're getting paid for it in some way," Anish said. "It's weird when talking to people. I don't necessarily call myself an athlete because I feel like that gives out a misperception of what I do, but personally I see myself as an athlete."

And there's the pull—that pull between what the world sees us as and what we see ourselves as. The social definition of "athlete" doesn't always match up with our internal definition of "athlete." Anish, for example, sees herself as an athlete in a broader, more inclusive way than the world does. That was the definition of "athlete" I was striving for myself; I struggled to embrace that as I trained and raced and explored in an athletic world that prioritized *results* over *experience*.

Flipping the Script

I carefully measured each step. The trail had turned to bare rocks, mostly smooth and steep, while the wind seemed determined to blow me back. I was careful to plant my boot firmly and completely on the rock, to walk any cracks I could find and traverse when possible. The trail was marked with yellow paint blazes, but I worked more from cairn to cairn, finding the piles of stones created by hikers to help mark the trail. I forced my mind to focus on the next small task and not the ache in my legs or the rumbling in my stomach.

I was closing in to 5,343 feet, the summit of Mount Marcy, the highest point in New York State. Near. It had to be near. I had just walked through nearly all four seasons—a beautifully green forest trail that had a gentle, gradual climb, followed by a steeper grade, followed by snow packed still on the upper portions of the trail in late May. By the time I reached 5,000 feet, the snow was gone, but the mountain top was bare rock with wind gusts that knocked my socks off (figuratively, of course), and instilled just a little bit of fear in me. To be blown off the top of the highest peak in New York State . . . well, that seemed another stupid way to die.

I reached another pile of trail-marking stones. (These are called "cairns," as I learned the real backpacking lingo.) I paused to survey where I was and where I was headed. My friend and guide for the day, Tracy, came up beside me.

"See that plaque?" she asked, pointing to a historical marker embedded in the rock. "That's your summit."

Suddenly, I didn't need to concentrate so much on my footing. The wind gusts which I had feared would knock me over were now driving the fear out of me. For all intents and purposes, I sprinted to that plaque. I went right up to the rock, I placed my hands on its cool, smooth face, and I bent down and kissed it.

It was a spontaneous move. I didn't know how I would feel once I reached the summit of Mount Marcy, the highest peak in New York State. I had no grand gesture planned and no expectations. I had respect for the mountain and for the Adirondacks. I knew it would be hard and challenging. But I didn't go in with a metaphysical plan.

I went in with only one goal—to climb up the mountain and climb back down.

It was a year after I had submersed myself in the elusive sub-two-hour half-marathon goal. I was burnt out on goals. I was burnt out on track workouts and tempo-pace runs. I was burnt out from striving to be something; I was burnt out on having to prove I was an athlete to others and to myself.

Hiking Mount Marcy had long been on my bucket list, but I can't quite explain why. It's the place where Teddy Roosevelt intended to go the day he was summoned back to Buffalo to take the presidential oath of office after William McKinley died. I suppose that when history and nature collide, it becomes a natural curiosity for me.

Plus, there's the difficulty. Mount Marcy isn't the most difficult climb among the forty-six High Peaks in New York State, but it's the tallest and one of the longest, with a roundtrip of fifteen miles. The trail is not terribly technical, but erosion and foot traffic have worn it down; it's full of rocks, roots, and muck. (We had the added bonus of encountering three miles' worth of ice on the trail, which we weren't anticipating.) It's not an easy day hike, and part of me certainly wanted the challenge.

As I encountered more stories of women who hiked thousands of miles or climbed mountains—stories such as that of Heather "Annish" Anderson—I began to rethink my notion of an athlete as someone who only trains and competes, as someone who constantly tries to best her last time or win a coveted jar of almond butter as an age-group award winner. Maybe I'd always been an athlete. Maybe my love of hiking was my inner athlete's way of getting out to play.

Maybe I just didn't see myself for what I really was.

As I was drawn to this idea of hiking Mount Marcy, I started to research the trail. It seemed to take most people about eight hours. It sounded pretty well-marked, although the final stretch of scrambling over slabs of rock to the summit would be a bit confusing. All of my hiking had been on trails in state parks, not climbs to the tops of mountains. I'd never experienced following a trail above a tree line. With no trees, there would be no place to hang trail makers, those brightly colored circles with friendly stick-figured hikers to point the way. I was up for the challenge, but lacking in some technical skill. I emailed people in local hiking groups to ask for advice. I was scared out of my mind to try to do this by myself, but it seemed to be my only option, as all my triathlon and running friends were busy racing or training for races and just couldn't fit a weekend on a mountain into their schedule.

All but one, that is. My friend Tracy said she'd take me up the mountain and be my guide.

Tracy was an Ironman and distance runner. She'd also become a "46er" the previous summer once she'd summited all forty-six High Peaks in the Adirondack region of New York State, through a combination of hiking with her dad in her youth and spending two months of the summer polishing off her requirements. In May she and her dad ("Tough Guy" Tom) were headed to Lake Placid to receive their certificates at the annual Spring 46er Meeting. Tracy invited me to come along to Lake Placid with them and then to hike Mount Marcy the day after the awards dinner.

Break out the bucket list—I was about to cross one off! And I was ridiculously excited.

And nervous.

And then excited again.

I could not have been in better hands to tackle my first Adirondacks hike, not just in terms of their experience and Tom's vast knowledge of the woods and backcountry hiking but also from their positivity, zest for life, and complete patience.

Even with my excitement, my old negative self-talk emerged. Instead of doubting I could hike Mount Marcy, particularly now that I had experienced friends to travel with me, I doubted my motives. Instead of fearing the physical experience, I had thoughts that criticized my intentions. A bucket-list hike up Mount Marcy. Wasn't that cliché? Wasn't I just trying to search for meaning on the mountain like every other middle-aged woman who'd read the book *Wild* by Cheryl Strayed? Wasn't I just trying to knock off another experience to say I had done it, like the Ironman or the marathon?

But instead of simply believing those negative thoughts, I engaged with them. I countered them by listening to my gut. I'd started to learn that good things happened when I listened to my gut.

I wasn't interested in peak-bagging—the practice of putting as many mountain summits on your outdoor resume as possible—or even in becoming a 46er by hiking all the High Peaks in New York State. I did not expect the mountain to change me. Or save me. Or give me meaning. I didn't so much as want to *be seen on* the mountain as I wanted to *see* the mountain.

I wanted to experience the steep sections and rocks and roots and varying degrees of difficulty. Clearly the challenge was physical, but I wanted to challenge myself mentally, too, to work on staying present and performing to the best of my abilities instead of comparing myself to others.

This is exactly how I got myself in trouble when I felt the pressure of the group of college stewards hiking behind me on the descent of the mountain. Instead of pulling over and letting them pass, I tried to keep their pace. And I wiped out. Hard. It was the only time on the trail when I couldn't save myself from my stumbling feet. And I stumbled a lot. Tracy's dad told me I had about 4,000 near-misses. "Try to make it closer to a thousand," he told me. It was funny and kind, a reminder that I'm a better, more effective hiker when I take my time and go my own pace.

True on the trail. True in life.

In order to do this, I had to be mindful. I had to think about the terrain. I had to measure my own pace and be aware of my own energy level. I had to not worry about keeping *up* but rather keeping *upright*.

Sure, there are competitions on the trail—records for things like the fastest known thru-hikes and the fastest completion of the forty-six High Peaks in New York State. There are competitions and records for pretty much everything. But that's not my goal. My athletic life could be about more than traditional measures of competition. It could be deeper than personal bests. It could go beyond the outward trappings of a Boston Marathon qualifying time or a sub-two-hour half-marathon.

At the top of the mountain, I could see that I had always been on an athletic journey. Only I never gave myself permission to see myself as an athlete. As I kissed the plaque marking the summit of Mount Marcy, I let go of those preconceived notions, those constricting social definitions, and saw myself as I truly was.

A woman who, among other things, is an athlete.

Women Are on the Trails, Too

The pictures are breathtaking.

Some show views of mountain ranges stretching to infinity.

Some show snow-covered forests.

Some demonstrate the silent beauty of the desert, while others refresh the soul with shots of hidden lakes and streams.

In all seasons, on all terrain, Heather "Anish" Anderson takes her followers along the trail. They get to watch her document her training days, her weekend summits, and her record-setting thru-hikes via social media. It's not so much that she loves the attention or is seeking publicity; rather, she knows that by sharing her passion for hiking and the outdoors she can help inspire other women and perhaps help them move past the fear they've been unconsciously indoctrinated into as women in American society.

Anish is one of a few women to undertake fastest-known-time challenges on long, arduous backcountry trails (plus, she's even found that nearly all of the outdoor recreation material has been written by men). That's why she's committed to be active on social media, promoting her treks, day-hikes, and general outdoor adventures.

"When I started my first thru-hike, I had zero female role models to look at," Anish said. "Every book I read was written by a guy. All the pictures were of guys. You didn't hear about the women out there doing it.

Women were definitely a minority and didn't have much of a voice before the Internet.

"It wasn't until I was out hiking, running into other women and seeing them hiking, that I realized other women were doing the same thing. Most of the women were in groups or started out solo and ended up hiking with other people. It's not like it's a bad idea to go hike with other people, but I wanted women to realize they don't need to do that. They're coming from a place of fear, and usually it's a fear of being by yourself. There's nothing inherently more dangerous being out there as a woman."

That's the key phrase.

There's nothing inherently more dangerous being out there as a woman. And that's a topic other women have explored as well.

Everyday Acts of Bravery

There exists a built-in bias that women are somehow more at risk for bad things to happen to them simply because they are women. Girls are taught this growing up. Girls are taught to deal with risk by avoiding it or at least minimizing it. Girls are taught to avoid skinned knees and bruises. Girls are taught fear.

The messages come in subtle, well-intentioned ways. After all, what parent wants to see their child injured on the playground? But a study titled "Parental Influences of Toddler's Injury-Risk Behaviors: Are Sons and Daughters Socialized Differently?" published in the *Journal of Applied Developmental Psychology* in 1999 found that parents have a different way of operating for their sons versus their daughters. The study included a firehouse-type pole and found that parents encouraged their sons, gave them more direction and information on how to complete the task; but for their daughters they provided more physical assistance, less encouragement, and had increased perceptions of injury and vulnerability.

"What that's telling girls, and telling boys, is that girls are fragile and need our help," said Caroline Paul, who authored the book *The Gutsy Girl: Escapades for Your Life of Epic Adventure.* "Boys are taught bravery;

we, as girls and women, are taught to look through a lens of fear. If a girl doesn't want to do it, it's viewed as fine. But boys look at the challenge head-on. They assess the courage needed. They get out of their comfort zone. These are lessons boys learn early. Girls don't get these lessons, these really vital skills like resiliency and confidence and bravery."

When girls aren't encouraged to go outside their comfort zone on the playground, it can have implications for other areas of their life. That includes school, career, relationships. That includes sticking with sports in the middle-school years. That includes claiming an athletic identity despite not living up to the sport-ethic standards.

What's more, Caroline said, if girls—and later, women—never have the chance to practice bravery in daily life, they can miss the difference between fear and excitement.

"Fear and excitement feel very similar," Caroline said. "So for a lot of women who never practiced bravery, they don't recognize the difference between fear and exhilaration. Say they're mountain climbing and they feel something and they mistake it for overwhelming fear. It may be fear and excitement. It feels the same—a heightened heartbeat and your muscles are a little tense. If you don't practice bravery, you don't know the difference and you don't know yourself that well and you end up cutting yourself out of a lot of experiences because you think, 'Oh that's scary. That must be bad.' "

Fortunately, I had parents who would just hand me the bottle of Bactine when I scraped my knee during childhood-summer explorations. There were never any explicit instances of pulling me off playground equipment or telling me I couldn't do something because it was too dangerous for a girl.

Still, the societal messages seeped into my head and I found myself in many of life's experiences struggling to discern between fear and excitement. Am I holding back because there is real danger ahead? Or am I holding back because I immediately equate scary feelings with danger? Often I put artificial limits on myself under the guise of being "realistic." And while that has served me well at times, more often than not it has kept me from accepting challenges.

When I lean into my athletic identity, I see that it's not so much danger that I'm afraid of as it is failure. Realistically, can I run a sub-two-hour half-marathon? Maybe not. But what if I tried? What if I tried without being tied to the end result? What if I approached the training like this?

I'm going to shoot for a 1:59 half-marathon.

I'm going to work really hard.

I'm going to get to the start line, run my best today, and if I don't make it, that's OK.

Because I'll have challenged myself for weeks leading up to the day.

That one day doesn't define me, but the work I put in will challenge and change me.

For quite a while, I had allowed the results to define my worthiness as an athlete. But this new approach felt much more in line with what my inner athlete wanted. And to take this approach requires a little bravery. Because it wasn't what everyone else was doing.

Chapter 8: They Say It's a Man's World (But You Can't Prove That By Me)

Girls Are Still Second-Class Athletic Citizens

The players stood on the ice, wearing Team USA hockey jerseys over their street clothes—good for photo ops and identification by reporters. The local media was on hand to talk with the young women, all eighteen years old or under, in Buffalo to play for the International Ice Hockey Federation Women's World Junior Championship.

I was part of the media gaggle, asking questions about the tournament, about preparation, about expectations for the event. Nearly all of the players were on their way to play hockey at a Division I school. These were the best women's hockey players in the U-18 age group, the next generation of the Olympic team.

A reporter for a local television station which didn't regularly cover sports was the first to ask a question. "Tell me," he said, brow furrowed, body leaning slightly in. "Did you originally want to be a figure skater? And were your first skates figure skates?"

There's a solid chance I rolled my eyes, and I definitely looked at the young woman with my mouth turned down as if to somehow try to convey a non-verbal apology for the question that wasn't mine. *Please don't think we're all this backward in Buffalo.*

Inside, I was raging. RAGING! I was raging so much I couldn't form complete sentences in my head.

What the . . . ? Wait . . . what? For real? Did he . . . ? No. He— What?!

It was December 2014. And a reporter in a good-sized American city asked an elite women's hockey player if she at heart really wanted to be a *figure skater* instead.

To their credit, the seventeen-year-olds handled it with poise, giving a smile and a small laugh. No one really wanted to be a figure skater, but a few did start out with figure skates their first time on the ice. But you don't use toe-picks to play hockey, so they changed up pretty quickly. I was in awe at the way they handled the awkwardness.

Unfortunately, they may be used that.

There's a sense that women's athletics has "arrived" in the United States. Women's basketball is on television! They give out scholarships to girls! Female athletes win gold medals at the Olympics! They star in Gatorade commercials!

But the veneer of success is thinly veiled. Sport is still a gendered activity, and is presented in society as a very *male* realm. If you're a girl and play sports, you better be the best there ever was. And even if you are, it will take a long time to acknowledge, and we'll still try to knock you down by calling you too muscular, masculine, or questioning your commitment or validity as an athlete because you like to shop. And that's just the case of tennis great, Serena Williams.

Without question, there are more opportunities for girls and women to play sports. The federal legislation Title IX, which banned discrimination based on gender in school settings, created a new opening for athletic girls. In 1972, the year Title IX was passed, only 7 percent of high-school athletes were girls. By the 2010–11 academic year, girls accounted for 41 percent of all high-school athletes. Athletic budgets at colleges have also increased funding for women's sports, going from 2 percent of the athletic department's budget in 1972 to 34 percent in 2011.

That's some serious success.

Still, hold off printing that *Mission accomplished!* banner just yet.

By 2016, there were several versions of the Always Confidence & Puberty Survey which, among other things, looked at how high-school girls participated in sports, the role that societal pressure played in their decision-making, and the level of confidence they felt.

The survey found that 51 percent of girls quit spots by the age of seventeen. Of those who dropped out, seven out of ten felt they didn't belong in sports; overall, 67 percent believed that society does not encourage them to play sports.

So . . . yeah.

Alex Morgan, a phenomenal female soccer player, may have a high-profile commercial spot with Coca-Cola, but it's a drop in the bucket to counteract the messages girls and women receive daily about how they're supposed to act. And the measures of the sport ethic, the definition of athletes who are committed and strong and perhaps even bold in their language about it—that still doesn't fit with our expectations of women in American society.

Before you think you've evolved beyond the gender stereotypes, take a long look. Because you probably haven't. Charisse L'Pree is an assistant professor of communications at Syracuse University. She has her doctorate degree in Social Psychology. She studies how the media affects our identity, attitude, and behavior. It's her life's work. And yet even she catches herself performing gender in the subtle ways society teaches.

"Boy culture is about controlling your environment," Charisse said. "Girl culture is being considerate of other people's needs. We're socialized that way, and when you're socialized to do it you have a knee-jerk reaction. We all have to be aware that we can fall into the stereotypes. One of the things women are socialized to do is when a man looks at you, the moment you make eye contact you look away. It's coy and feminine and you're taught that you can't stare at a man."

And even Charisse, with her knowledge and research and understanding of gendered socialization, catches herself sometimes looking away instead of looking directly into a man's face.

"As women, we are socialized to be considerate of others, often at the expense of ourselves," Charisse said. "What women do instead of bragging is 'humble brag.' It's bragging, but you have to be humble about it. Women don't want to brag, so they'll say, 'Oh I guess I have to tell you.'

"When I'm teaching a class, I have to tell you I went to MIT for my undergraduate. The instinct is to drop it and move on. I'm not supposed to tell them these things. They might think I'm being arrogant or trying to show off. But no, I did that and it was awesome. I went to one of the top schools in the country."

This applies to the academic world—particularly fields of science, technology, engineering, and math—as well as the athletic world. Sport is still drawn as a masculine activity. The biases are not as overt as when the women who wanted to run long distances before 1972 were told by medical doctors that they would damage their reproductive systems and their uterus may fall out. But the biases still exist, enough to cause girls to drop out of sports and hold women back from embracing an identity of *athlete*, instead couching what they do in apologetic terms.

As a fierce feminist and proponent of women's rights and the women's sports movement, I can be bold and brash in my opinions. I'm not a shrinking violet. But chances are if you go for a run with me I'll say, "Sorry I'm so slow. I hope I'm not holding you back."

It's all the social conditioning that Charisse and others have researched. I'm more concerned with other people's needs, with making them happy, with apologizing for something which requires no apology. Maybe I'm not running that pace right now. Maybe this is supposed to be my easy run, and that pace is too hard. Maybe that pace is something I never achieve, outside a five-second interval on the treadmill. But my instinct, my knee-jerk reaction, is to put the other people in the group first and to apologize for my (perceived) lack of skill.

No wonder it's so difficult to say out loud, with confidence and conviction: *I AM AN ATHLETE.* There's no humble bragging in that. But if I said, "Well, you know, I did an Iron Distance triathlon and six marathons . . . but I wasn't very fast," that would put my accomplishment into the world only with a very diminutive delivery, which undermines the accomplishment.

Especially within my own mind.

Why Would a *Girl* Be a Sportswriter?

Growing up, I encountered few overt messages of female inferiority. I don't remember any time being told flat-out I couldn't do something because I was a girl. I don't remember being openly discouraged to try something. I don't remember being expressly schooled in the "humble brag" or the feminine mystique of diminishing oneself so as to not look haughty or aggressive or full of myself.

But those messages were all still there.

It started in elementary school, when we had a male student-teacher who was a big sports fan. Remember this story? He took one of my male classmates aside and they used math to figure out the Major League Baseball standings. Every day they'd pore over the newspaper sports page and work out mathematical problems thanks to the New York Yankees and Philadelphia Phillies. I wasn't included, despite the fact that I loved baseball, that I listened to it all the time on my grandparents' porch in the summer.

I felt like an outsider. Like those were two things I wasn't supposed to like—baseball and math. Perhaps if math were presented to me in this way, I wouldn't have grown up assuming I was bad at math and then living up to that assumption. Mostly I didn't care about the math; I cared about the baseball, about sports, and was silently hurt that I wasn't included in the baseball-standings math clique.

It was also the first time I can recall not being included in a sports discussion. Maybe I wasn't supposed to like baseball either? Thankfully my home was one filled with passionate sports fans, most importantly my mother and grandmother. It never occurred to me that women couldn't know as much about sports as men.

This came as a surprise to many of the men I met in my first years as a sports reporter.

When asked what I did for a living, I would respond with "I'm a sportswriter."

Some guys (and they were always guys) were slightly impressed, but most incredulous.

"Your dad must have played sports," they would say.

Nope. I mean, my dad was active—he taught me how to ice skate and ride a bike; he took me hiking—but he spent more time mowing the lawn on Sunday afternoons than watching football.

"You must have had older brothers, then," they would respond.

Nope. A younger brother. Four years younger. So as kids, he more often than not followed my lead.

"Uncles, then? Uncles who played?" they'd ask, grasping for anything.

Nope.

"Then how did you become interested in sports?" they'd ask.

My mother and my grandmother, I would tell them. My mother and grandmother were the huge sports fans in my family. They were the ones who watched carefully, who made as many comments as my grandfather and uncle. They were invested. They were knowledgeable.

And that's when the men who questioned how a girl would become a sports reporter usually walked away.

The assumptions were obvious. I had to have been influenced by a male role model in my life to become interested in sports. But more than that, there had to be a *reason* that I became interested in sports and wanted to be a sports writer. Did they ever ask men who were sports writers how they came to be interested in sports? As far as I knew, I was the only person in the press box who had to deal with these questions, because 99 percent of the time I was the only female working as a reporter in the press box.

What You Do Matters, Even When You Don't Think It Does

Aside from questioning how I, a girl, could ever get interested in sports, the other way my place in the sports-reporting world was questioned came through trivia contests.

Those I shut down pretty quickly.

I'm not good at trivia. I don't remember a lot of names, dates, or other random statistical information. That's not how my brain is wired. The only names and dates I've retained are from rhymes my study partners and I would create when studying for AP History tests (*The Magna Carta/ in 1215/ King John, he signed it/ 'cause he was mean*). I don't know who won the American League batting title in 1963. When I started my career, in the pre-Internet days, there was always the handy sports almanac which had all the information I could ever need. Now you can just Google it, and right from the comfort of the phone, which is probably in your hand right now. (P.S. Carl Yastrzemski won the American League batting title in 1963. Thanks, BaseballReference.com!)

Stats never drove my love of sports. It was the stories. It was the sense of family and community. That's what hooked me. That's what I fell in love with.

Traditionally these are viewed as "soft" traits and "feminine" traits. Boys excel in math. Girls excel in English. From the beginning, I preferred story over stats. I approached my job looking for the best stories, not looking to showboat my sports knowledge. Sports, at its heart, is about people. So I wrote more about people than I did about a team's defensive-zone strategy or the shot selection in an offensive scheme, although not writing about strategy or statistics or trendy analytics made me less credible in the eyes of some. The criticism usually came from readers, but occasionally came from colleagues as well. Sometimes they were trying to be helpful. Most of the time I internalized it as my doing a poor job.

There were times when I tried to write more like the guys, particularly in the immediate aftermath of a talking-to from an editor who offered plenty of criticism but no suggestions on how to get better—other than to try to be more like the other reporters, who were all old white guys and writing from an old-white-guy perspective. Still, I tried to follow their lead. After all, they were successful, and I wanted to be successful, and if this was the way to success I might as well follow the well-worn path.

I specifically applied this to any assignment that involved women's sports. The beginning of my career still included a pervasive attitude of "Gee! Girls? Playing *sports?* No way!" Coverage of women's sports was more novelty than news. I was warned by well-intentioned friends in the industry against being pigeonholed as the "women's-sports reporter." I needed to cover men's sports. Football if at all possible (because it doesn't get much more stereotypically masculine than football).

But I knew first-hand from working in both high school and college as a basketball manager the amount of talent these women possessed and the work they put into their sport. They deserved media coverage as much as their male counterparts. So I covered women's sports and wrote about women athletes like the men wrote about men's sports—with plenty of analysis and stats (and just a smidgen of personality when warranted).

For this effort I received email after email from readers who couldn't believe the newspaper was wasting ink on covering women's sports.

So much for legitimizing the women's sports movement to our readers.

Meanwhile, my own writing was getting too formulaic. It felt clumsy. It felt unnatural. I wasn't loving what I was writing. I was stressed and unsure of myself. Writing like the guys was getting me nowhere. I returned to what I felt I did best in the newspaper world: tell stories about people, using numbers to help illustrate a point when necessary. Sports are played by people and while their skills may seem superhuman, they are not bound to follow a statistical formula.

Somehow—and I'm still not sure how this happened—I convinced my editors to send me to Minnesota to cover the inaugural Women's Frozen Four, the first ice hockey championship for women sponsored by the NCAA. I say I'm unsure how I convinced my editors because, well, there were no local teams in the event; there weren't even any local players . . . nothing remotely connected Buffalo or Western New York to the NCAA championship. They were probably sick of my constantly pushing for women's sports coverage—if I was out of state, they couldn't hear me complain that much.

I went for three days, gathered a number of stories about the growth of women's hockey, about the first-ever national championship, and, of course, covering the games (including semifinals, third-place game, and championship). Minnesota–Duluth won the first title, and then the next two.

Back in Buffalo, I was pretty excited about my stories, and they earned a central spread in Monday's paper, the day after the title game. This was a big deal!

Only ... no one said anything to me about it. Not one person commented on my work (with the exception of my mom and grandfather, who always said how much they loved every word I write). There wasn't even one comment on the historic nature of the event. There were a few emails, however, asking why *The Buffalo News* bothered to send someone to Minnesota to cover women's hockey, because no one cares about women's hockey. I was starting to get numb to that criticism.

Then came the phone call.

I was in the office, which is not a regular occurrence in our sports department as we're usually out at games and practices and writing our stories on-site or at home. But here I was in the office, and someone had called asking for me. *This can't be good,* I thought. *No one knows I'm here and I'm not expecting a call.* I braced myself and picked up the phone.

"Sports, this is Amy," I said.

It was a woman on the other end of the phone. After confirming I was the person who wrote the stories about women's college hockey, she started to tell me her story.

Her daughter played hockey, but since the high schools didn't sponsor teams, she played for one of the local club organizations, made up of girls from a number of different high schools. The team had just won a really big tournament, she said. But in the morning announcements during homeroom when they congratulated the performance of the school's teams, her accomplishment was left out.

"No one cares," her daughter had told her, despondent and near tears.

That's when her mom picked up the paper and saw a huge layout about women's hockey with multiple stories and photos.

"That's not true," her mom said. "Look at the paper! See! People care about women's hockey! They care about what you're doing."

It was a happy coincidence that my stories about the NCAA championship appeared at the exact time this high-school girl was struggling with feelings of hurt and loneliness. Or maybe it wasn't a coincidence at all, but the universe aligning everything in the right time and space.

Regardless, I was happy.

For the first time I had tangible proof that what I wrote made a difference.

I'd been warned by well-intentioned men in the field to be wary of being pigeonholed as a "women's sports writer," lest I be relegated to covering all the women and girls' sports, trapped in a sort of pink ghetto with high tops and ponytails. I appreciated the sentiment. I understood what they meant. I knew they were trying to help my career, to keep me focused on doing work which would get me noticed and move me up the ladder.

But for the first time, I really stopped to consider what I wanted.

What I wanted was to somehow make a difference, to give a voice to people who normally don't get one—and in the sports pages, those voices overwhelming belong to women.

I didn't paint myself into a corner. I still covered plenty of men's sports. But every time there was an opportunity to cover women's sports, I did my best to be on the story.

Because I'd quickly learned that if I didn't do it, no one would.

The Elites Are Just Like You and Me

It would be seven years after covering the first Women's Frozen Four before I plunged into the icy waters of Keuka Lake for my first triathlon. And while I had started to come into my own voice as a reporter, it became stronger when I tapped into the resources of my own athletic identity.

Performance is shaped by so many variables—a reality I was learning through my own athletic pursuits. I saw my own training fluctuate depending on various elements. Was I hydrated? Did I drink enough water? Did I get enough sleep? How was my nutrition, both in my daily diet and around my endurance sessions? Was I stressed about a sick relative? Was I too sore from the previous day's workout for my body to move effectively? Was I mentally off my game, listening to the ad hoc negative committee meeting inside my head, telling me that I sucked? Was I comparing myself too harshly with others or to some arbitrary standard I had set for myself?

All these things could impact my day in a variety of ways. And the same was true for the elite athletes I was writing about. We all dealt with hydration and nutrition. We all balanced hard work with rest and recovery. We all battled negative thoughts. The only difference was a matter of scale.

I started to notice how the elite athletes I wrote about trained. I started to ask questions about nutrition and strength training. I paid more attention to sports science studies and wrote entire stories about the impact of sleep on an athlete's performance—sleep which can be difficult for, say, hockey players to get when they're playing five games in seven days and traveling to three different cities back and forth between two time zones. (I received surprisingly good feedback for that story, which was interesting and timely and off the beaten path.)

The more I followed what interested me—instead of following some script of what I thought I was supposed to be writing—the more I enjoyed my work. Occasionally this would bring me a nice pat on the back and an "Atta girl!" from the higher ups, which was welcomed but no longer my objective. Pink ghetto? Pigeon-holed? I started to care less about the labels. And yet, there was one label I was still after—*athlete*.

Creating My Own Definition

There is a line in the song "Do Right Woman, Do Right Man" by Aretha Franklin that I particularly love:

"They say that it's a man's world, but you can't prove that by me."

It's been a line I've returned to over and over again as a woman in sports media. While there are more and more women in the field, it's still dominated by men. Diversity of all kinds is lacking in the sports media, and when you're the only woman in the room it can be exhausting. Once, a male sports writer began ranking who had the most "bodacious boobs" in the press box.

Did he not know I was there?

(And thank God he didn't bring up *my* name.)

There are other times when the conversation isn't sexist but instead inane, usually centering on social media trolls and how right the writers are and how wrong the fans are. It makes me smile a bit. The vitriol these guys get on Twitter is nothing compared to the emails I used to get questioning my place in the press box, suggesting I just wanted to see naked men, talking about the lesbians who play sports and wondering if I was pushing some sort of liberal lesbian agenda.

Seriously. I've been asked that. More than once.

Sports is a man's world. But you can't prove that by me. Or by the other women I know who are fearlessly pursuing their passion, ignoring the crap that guys say. Or the way guys approach sports. The very masculine-based sports ethic, which helps us define our social definition of an athlete, leaves little room for things like, oh, play.

Sports are a serious undertaking. Sports are not *play*. It's a business, from the pros with million-dollar contracts to the sports apparel industry which make millions off the weekend 5K runners. It's competition. It's about getting better. It's about mileage and new gadgets and getting a leg up on the rest of the field.

I like getting better. I like some competition—the kind that pulls me forward to be a better version of myself, not the kind that constantly compares my journey to someone else. I like new running gear and trying the latest gizmos and energy gels. But you know what else I like?

Play.

This does not fit the "man's world" version of sports, unless you're talking about five-year-olds—and even then, "play" can be an iffy way to categorize sports.

But that's what I like to do. I like to play. I like to explore, and for me that means challenging my own limits, seeing what I can do, how far I can go, and how fast I can push myself. To me, being an athlete means being true to myself, to my unique athletic calling which includes training and competition, but still keeping my big-picture in mind—to be healthy and fit and strong enough to do the things which ignite my soul. To be able to hike up a mountain, jump in a kayak, or ride my bike through gently rolling hills. To be able to see a new adventure and dip into an established well of bravery, one that I've built through practice and numerous dry-heave-inducing training runs done at a steady tempo pace.

There have been well-meaning men in my life who have told me otherwise. They told me that I need to be more focused and dedicated. I need to set goals—real, tangible goals, they emphasized—and achieve them. For starters, I should work on running a respectable 5K time. If I'm not going to take this seriously, then it's probably best if I step away.

A lot of well-meaning men have given me a lot of advice, from how to be a sports reporter to how to be a runner.

It was time for me to create my own definition, one that was not only big enough to include my goals but actually celebrated my goals, no matter how amorphous they sounded to others.

Athletics may be a man's world, you see, but you can't prove that by me. Not any more.

Chapter 9: Vertical and Breathing

Entering the Weight Room

I quickly lost track of how many times I said "I'm sorry" and moved out of the way.

The gym was effective but compact. Bring in a team of twelve people and suddenly it felt crowded. Me? I was just trying to get in my workout, following the plan written by my trainer which included more work with weights, dumbbells, and pushups than I had ever done in my life.

I wasn't a novice to strength training. I'd dabbled in it before, working with a fellow runner who was getting a certification to be a strength coach for a few months and occasionally hitting the machines at the big box-store gym. Intellectually, I knew that strength training was important for both performance and my overall health, but I balked at it.

Because I wasn't strong.

A triathlete friend of mine had fallen mad, crazy-in-love with CrossFit. He tried to get me to try it. Instead I used my yoga practice as strength training, arguing to him—and myself—that I just wasn't strong enough to do CrossFit. I had no upper body strength. Zero. Zilch. I had heard about the workouts and knew there was no way I would be able to perform the exercises, let alone survive an entire workout. I readily admitted I was completely intimidated by CrossFit. Maybe if I got stronger I could try it, I told him (and myself).

As if I needed to be good at it before I even tried it. Hadn't I been through this ridiculous logic? How can you learn something new if you think you need to be perfect at it before you even start? And why was I balking at the same truth I spoke of to others—that everyone needs to start somewhere, that you start where you are and where you are right now is already just fine.

Still intimidated—mostly by videos of yelling instructors (I was never motivated by someone yelling at me)—yet intrigued by the benefits of strength training, I began to be curious about other options.

Meanwhile, my job as a sports reporter put me regularly on the hockey beat and I spent a lot of time in the newly built HarborCenter in downtown Buffalo—a facility with two rinks that quickly became a favorite venue for USA Hockey events, college teams, and the occasional practice for the NHL's Buffalo Sabres. It was there I ran across a gym called Impact.

Actually, it doesn't even call itself a gym. The trainers there specialize in working with athletes to get better at their respective sports. I was intrigued. It seemed like a good way to add some strength training to my running and triathlon training. And it provided me the chance to work one-on-one with a coach, something I had been missing for the better part of a year (I had stopped working with my triathlon coach because I had no concrete goals and was in the process of buying my first house). I had enough knowledge base and saved workouts to create my own training plan, so I felt I did just fine. But I missed the interaction with a coach. I missed the reinforcement, the knowledge, the corrections to guide me back on track when I wandered off.

The sports performance center was at the heart of Buffalo's hockey universe. I would physically be here a lot for work—might as well give their programming a try and combine work with workouts, right?

That's how I found myself on the thirty-yard turf track, apologizing to another athlete.

It was June and I was about two months into my strength training workouts. I'd been coming two days a week, working one day with my trainer and the other day on my own. I was slowly building my strength with squats and chest presses and glute bridges and planks. The other athletes in the gym were younger, more fit, and able to put massive amounts of weight at the end of their barbells. Meanwhile, I was trying to press ten pounds over my head, quietly in the corner so as not to disturb the people doing "real" work.

A cluster of people was on the strip of turf track that day. I was trying to get in my workout as inconspicuously as possible, but every time I turned around someone was coming toward me, lugging a weight or pushing a sled or doing something that looked totally badass.

"I'm sorry"—I said this about a dozen times in quick succession. I wasn't even apologizing for anything specific; I was apologizing for taking up space, for pretending to be an athlete when I couldn't lift a quarter of the weight everyone else was.

"I'm sorry," I said again under my breath.

"Hey, we're all here for the same reason," one of the trainers said as he heard my fifteenth apology of the day. "We're all just trying to get better."

Cue the lightbulb moment.

I had fallen in love with this sports performance center because they treated everyone the same. Pro athlete, Division I athlete, elite travel teams, runners, those who just wanted to be in shape for their life . . . we all were treated as athletes. We all were after the same thing—to be a bit better than yesterday, to work on our weaknesses, to build on our strengths, and to move our body through space and time. Everything else, the level at which we were working at or toward, were just details.

What a revolutionary and freeing thought.

It's cliché to say that strength training has helped me become stronger not just physically but mentally and emotionally as well. I can't help that it's a cliché, but I can say it's unequivocally true. The weight room became a safe space for me. I was treated like an athlete, so it became easier for me to call myself an athlete.

And I was lifting barbells and pushing sleds with forty-five-pound plates on them—and did I mention I progressed to be able to do full-body pushups? I couldn't do any of that when I first started. That's because I had never done any of it before. You start where you are. You start at your beginning, and over time you create a new story for yourself.

The gym became the first place for me where failure was not just an option, but a celebrated one. I'd work with my trainer and he'd ask if I could go heavier.

"I don't know, but I'll try," I said.

"That's all I ask," was his reply.

Sometimes I cleared the weight. Sometimes I didn't. But I wouldn't know if I could lift a heavier weight unless I tried it, unless I challenged myself, unless I sunk into the belief that it's OK if it's hard and it hurts. Failure meant I had found my current max. It was not the end-game but rather a marker of where I was and where I could go.

I started talking about strength training with my friend BeeLynn, who competed in Strongman competitions and coached other women.

"We have to realize it's OK to take up space," she said. "Women come in saying 'Oh, I'm not that strong. I don't know if I can do that. I'm not strong enough for this.' Over time they start to internalize that message. But there is no 'strong enough to do this.' It's wherever you're at. It's where you start. I don't even like to hear the words 'I'll try' because that has the connotation that you won't be able to do it. They shift from being unsure of what they can do to surprising themselves with what they can do."

I started surprising myself in the weight room. I started to see myself as an athlete. More importantly, I started to think about what I wanted from my identity as an athlete. Time-based performance goals felt artificial, and they were frustrating and limiting me instead of inspiriting me.

So I took my newfound strength, loaded up my car, and drove eight hours to Williamson, West Virginia, to reframe my athletic identity at one of the toughest marathons in the country.

Pure Joy Over 26.2 Horribly Painful Miles

At the pre-race meeting in the Belfry High School auditorium, the race director said there were only two rules:

1. Try to finish before dark, because that's when most of the shootings and hangings occur.
2. If you see a pig, look the other way.

The rules make more sense if you know a bit about the infamous Hatfield-McCoy feud, which allegedly started with a dispute over a hog in 1878 and included violence, murder, and other mayhem on the West Virginia-Kentucky border. It's become a source of interest for history buffs and the curious, and some small communities celebrate that history while encouraging tourism with a bit of humor and lot of southern Appalachian flair.

I had been searching out races for 2015 and remember seeing the Hatfield-McCoy Marathon somewhere—perhaps flipping through a running magazine or scrolling through an Internet link on the best bucket-list marathons. Regardless of how it came into my consciousness, I decided I was in.

The race boasts of its ranking as one of the fifteen toughest marathons in the world by The Weather Channel. It makes the list for its hills, heat, and humidity. And if you didn't have much humility when you started, you found it in spades along the course.

The marathon begins in Kentucky and finishes in West Virginia, crossing the Tug River five times with 1,200 feet of climbing over the 26.2 miles. The toughness didn't lure me in and of itself. But the toughness of the course did create an atmosphere that I needed, that I craved, that I had never experienced at any other race in my life.

To start with, the race had no time limit.

No. Time. Limit.

That is highly unusual. In fact, I've never heard of another marathon without a time limit. Streets need to be re-opened to traffic, aid stations can only be staffed and stocked for so long, and race directors have a limited budget to pay police and emergency crews.

But Williamson, West Virginia, and the surrounding towns go all in to support the marathon. While I was excited about the whole no-time-limit, which took all the pressure off the race, I was concerned about the aid stations. Specifically, I was concerned they would be empty or closed by the time I got to the ones later in the race. So I questioned one of the volunteers at packet pick-up.

ME: I know there's no time limit, but how long do the aid stations stay open?

VOLUNTEER: They stay open the whole time.

ME: They *all* do? I'm slower, and I know sometimes stations close up or run out of stuff.

VOLUNTEER: No, ma'm. We stay open until the last runner goes by. The very last runner.

The volunteer pulled his shoulders back and puffed out his chest slightly, proud of the fact that they service *all* runners. And sure enough, while I was on the second half of the course, I saw a number of ATVs making their way from aid station to aid station to replenish supplies. The race director had said during the pre-race meeting that more than 700 volunteers would be on the course to help the 1,000 runners.

Seven hundred volunteers.

I felt loved and cared for. I felt as if all these people wanted me to succeed. Total strangers were cheering for me. As were all the other runners.

The pre-race pasta dinner held at the local school gave me a chance to meet other runners. A good number had done the race before and told stories about what to expect on the course to the newbies. All the while something struck me: no one was talking about a Boston qualifying time or a personal best. No one was even talking about pace.

No one.

Not a soul.

Every previous marathon I went to (whether I was running the full or the half) people were talking about getting their BQ—the ultimate mantle for a distance runner, qualifying for the famed 26.2 miles that ends in downtown Boston. Other races had people talking about PRs (personal records), with pace charts taped to their arms so they could make sure they're on track to run the time they want.

Time, time, time. It was all about the time.

But not at Hatfield-McCoy. No one was talking about time because time at this race was irrelevant and everyone knew it.

In the past I'd chosen some challenging races because I needed to beat the hell out of my body. I was in emotional pain one year—my relationship with my boyfriend had ended the day I found out my dad had prostate cancer. I needed hard races. I craved them. I needed the punishing training for my body to feel the way my insides did. It wasn't punishment but rather a need to match my insides with my outsides. The challenging races gave me an opportunity to release all that emotion—the pain, anger, sadness, and frustration—in the most productive way I knew.

But this challenge wasn't about the "hard." This was about the journey. This was about getting back to my athletic roots—of reveling in the process, of seeking adventure and seeing just how far I could go. It was about reconnecting with an athletic community that was more supportive than competitive. Only a hard race which by nature eschewed talk of PRs and BQs would give me that.

I accepted the gift with gratitude (also while sweat-soaked). When the shotgun went off for the 7 a.m. start, the temperature was already approaching 80 degrees and the humidity was clinging to my body. Oh, and at Mile 7 you climb "Blackberry Mountain," which gains 500 feet in one mile.

Yeah. That was not fun.

Even the other side made me cry as the steep downhill pitch pushed my toes into the front of my sneakers so hard I thought they were going to break through the shoe and force me to run the rest of the race with flip-flop-style kicks. (Luckily that didn't happen.)

Since I decided this race was about the journey and not the time, I took pictures on the course. At one point we passed a house with people sitting on lawn chairs, waving and clapping while their mini horses were in their front yard. Yes, people, I said MINI HORSES—how could I *not* stop? I went over with this young woman I had met at the pasta dinner and we took each other's picture in front of the mini horses. That may have been the coolest thing I've ever seen on a race course. I didn't care that it cost me two minutes. *Mini horses on the course*, people!

The halfway point of the race was in Matewan, West Viriginia. Emotionally, this was a difficult point. There weren't a lot of spectators cheering on the slower marathoners. Most of the people there were for the half-marathon and the people who ran the half-marathon were done.

If I had run the half-marathon, I'd be done. Why can't I be done? I thought.

No, I told myself. *Banish the thought. Must press on.*

The second half began on a trail that followed the river. Actually, I think it was a road, not a trail, but it was narrow and small. My mental capacities were starting to fade and an ambulance was now following me. It was getting hot and suddenly we were not running in the shade of the mountains anymore. We were in bright sun and it was punishing my body. Jumping in the river felt like a plausible plan.

It was around Mile 16 when I started to get hungry. Like, *starving*. An energy gel was not gonna cut it. And just like a miracle oasis in a desert, there was an aid station. And this one had grapes. GRAPES! Never was I so happy to see a Dixie cup filled with fruit. I also asked to stick my hands into their pool of ice. One of the volunteers suggested I shove ice down the back of my shorts. Brilliant! By the time I finished the race I had ice cubes and sponges shoved into all kinds of places on my person.

Did I mention at this point it was about 127 degrees with 200 percent humidity?

The final eight miles were fairly wide open. Not much shade, few clouds, no wind. The heat started to get to me and I slowed down. Considerably. I was expecting this. My legs were tired, but felt good. My lungs were OK. So why couldn't I run more? Waves of frustration would come then quickly pass, usually as I came to a water-stop filled with friendly folks or chatted with another runner.

One fellow runner asked if I saw the moonshine at the last water-stop. Nope. I missed it. He didn't. He saw it and asked about it. Then he had a shot. Then a guy brought out "strawberry-shine" and he had another shot. "I had about three shots of moonshine back there," the guy said. "I may be drunk by the end of the race."

At Mile 22 I started talking with a woman who was power-walking. She wished the water-stops had salt tablets.

"Hey, I've got one salt tablet left!" I said. "Do you want it?"

"It's your last one, are you sure?" she asked.

It was my spare salt tablet and it was all hers. I hope it helped.

With all the talk of the 500 feet gained at Mile 7 on Blackberry Mountain, it was easy to forget about Mile 23. The hill was not as steep, but still a struggle, and felt like the cruelest hill of them all. And yet in my head I knew that meant the end was near.

"Is this the last water-stop?" I asked shortly after leaving the last hill behind.

"No," said the woman who handed me my twenty-third cup of Gatorade that day. "You have one more. And then there's the Dairy Queen."

Ah, yes. The Dairy Queen. I had heard people talk about this at the pasta dinner. The last mile of the course turns onto the highway (or the "four-lane," as the locals call it) and passes a bunch of fast-food chains, including the glorious DQ. From what I was told, many people go in and buy ice cream for that last mile. While I rarely give up the opportunity for ice cream, I was too close to the finish line. The ice cream could wait.

Two turns later I was on Second Avenue in downtown Williamson. The finish line was in sight. I ran, fairly strong, to the end, greeted back home by Devil Anse Hatfield and Randall McCoy (well, actors playing the roles of Devil Anse and Randall).

I had a huge smile on my face.

But that wasn't the end of it. I collected my medal and my post-race swag, grabbed a red solo cup filled with beer, and walked back to the finish line. I found a seat a few hundred yards from the finish and cheered for the runners who were coming into town. I sat for about an hour with a woman who had finished the half-marathon and was waiting for her husband who was running the full marathon. We talked about the course, about the heat and humidity of the day, and how we both struggled. We clapped for runners who came by. Some were walking at this point. Didn't matter. We told them they were awesome. Because they were. We knew their pain. We knew how difficult this day was, how unrelenting the course could be. They had made it. We were genuinely proud to share our finisher medals with them.

Never have I felt more welcomed, more accepted. Never before have people looked at me and just assumed I was in town to run the marathon. "Oh, you must be a runner," they said. No one had ever come up to me before and told me that, and no one has done that since. It's a special bond I have with the people of this region, a community which provided the bright light I needed to embrace my own athletic identity. No longer was I discovering my "inner athlete." She was fully integrated into my being.

Finally, I had my definition of what it meant be an athlete. Finally, I allowed that definition to apply to myself.

Showing Up

Women have some pretty clever definitions of what it means to be an athlete.

"You know when you go into a gym and take a tour with a trainer and they ask you what your goals are? I tell them my goal is simple—to avoid atrophy," said Tara, who runs educational outdoor adventure trips for women.

"My definition of an athlete is vertical and breathing. If you're vertical and still breathing, you're an athlete," noted my friend Carolyn, whom I met during the Women's Quest cycling tour in Italy. She also gave me this next definition, which was the one I was looking for all along:

"It's all about showing up and being willing to put ourselves to the test, whether you show up for a race or for your life," Carolyn said. "I mean, what's the difference? Aren't we all athletes? Aren't we all taking what abilities we have and using them? It's about showing up for your life. That's being an athlete. That's game on."

On my wall are loads of race medals, mostly finisher medals from half-marathons, marathons, and a few long-distance triathlon events. Some days it sounds like I'm chasing bling, but really I'm not. I could take each medal down and tell you a story about the race, the venue, the city, and the people around me that day. I could tell you even better stories about the races that went wrong, with horrible weather conditions, physical ailments, or missed goals. The races where the wheels came off? Those were the ones with the most bang for my storytelling buck. The races where everything went perfectly? Boring and slightly predictable. But I can still take that medal off the wall and tell you its story.

My journey as an athlete continues and it's an ever-evolving one. My interest in triathlon took a backseat to distance for a while, simply because running fit in better with my schedule. Strength training continues to be a constant, but yoga has become more important. I'm more relaxed about my running schedule when it comes to fitting in other activities—like hiking or kayaking or taking an easy bike ride with friends.

Goals change, from race to race and from season to season. Sometimes I'm working for a personal best in a race, while sometimes I'm all about strength over speed. Sometimes my training is spot on for a PR, only to have race day bring uncontrollable factors into the mix—heat and humidity or cold rain or wind or the dreaded onset of your stomach no longer able to pleasantly accept and process sports drink and gels.

For me, being an athlete is about being fit and ready for adventure. It's about pushing myself out of my comfort zone. It's about being proud to take up space, to say "I am here and I am strong." It's about setting goals to guide the process but defining myself by achievements.

Being an athlete, you see, is really about being authentically myself and showing up for my own life.

When Mom Crossed the Finish Line

It was a warm July day and I knew when I got out of bed that morning that this 5K race was not going to be my finest moment. I was in the early stages of half-marathon training and the previous day I'd done a long run. I felt every yard of that twelve-miler in my legs that morning and quickly decided the Run Jimmy Run Charity 5K would be all about effort, not about pace.

But there was something much more important to me than a 5K. More important than pacing or placing. More important even than effort and showing up.

It was that my mom had a bib number for the first time and was lining up for the one-mile walk.

About five years earlier, she was diagnosed with non-Hodgkin's lymphoma (NHL) and COPD. After rounds of chemotherapy treatment and scans and follow-ups, she beat that cancer. Ironically, getting lymphoma probably saved her life. A follow-up scan showed her lymphoma gone, but caught a lesion in her lung. She was diagnosed with early-stage lung cancer.

Had it not been for that scan, doctors would probably never have caught the lung lesion. And by the time they did, it would have been too late to do anything about it.

With lots of fear and doubt and about a million other emotions, my mom picked a treatment course and got good news: the lesion responded to the treatment just as they had hoped.

Now, the treatment didn't make breathing any easier for her—she still struggled with her lungs and COPD. She struggled with her legs, the aftereffects of her lymphoma chemotherapy that lingered. But when my mom saw that the Run Jimmy Run Charity 5K registration was open, she asked if I was signing up.

Because, she told me, she was signing up for the walk. There were many options for her first official participation in a race. But this was the one she had to do first.

The race is in memory of the late Buffalo mayor, Jimmy Griffin, who was instrumental in getting the city a downtown ballpark. The race begins and ends at Buffalo's baseball stadium—and, as you know, baseball holds a special place in my mom's heart.

She grew up with Buffalo Bisons baseball in similar fashion to me, hearing her parents talk about the old games at Offermann Stadium and heading to games herself. Baseball is a place where she still connects with them, still hears their voices. It's a place beyond description, a place of the heart, a place that, if you've seen the movie *Field of Dreams*, you may find familiar.

So this had to be her first official walk.

Mom had been tracking her steps for months. She was ready for this. I gave my parents fist-bumps at the start line and took off on my 5K run while they were at the back of the pack. And I mean the *back* of the pack. The walkers were mostly power-walkers; my parents are not power walkers, and they quickly lost the group. Washington Street, where the race begins, is an uphill. Mom wasn't mentally prepared for that. Early on, she thought she couldn't do it. She thought she'd have to turn back.

Nevertheless, she persisted.

She and my dad made it to City Hall, took a break, then started making their way back to the ballpark. By the time she crossed the finish line, a little off the course, she had walked 1.6 miles.

I found her as she was approaching her first finish line.

I was jumping up and down.

I was cheering at the top of my lungs.

Because that, my friends, was amazing.

Take *that*, lung cancer!

When my mom crossed the finish line, it wasn't the end of something but rather the beginning. A few days before the walk she confided to me: "I'm at the age where, if I want to do something, I'm just going to do it," she told me. "It might take me longer with some things, but I'm not going to let things stop me from doing what I want."

Trust me, my mother would never label herself an athlete. But what she did—setting a challenging goal, putting in work, pushing back mental and emotional demons, showing up and doing the best she could—that's pretty much what being an athlete boils down to.

And I'm pretty sure my grandmother was watching somewhere, screaming "You're nuts!" while beaming with pride.

I don't know if there's an age requirement for living how you want, but I'm going to follow my mom's lead.

The worst that could happen . . . well, the worst rarely happens.

And when something akin to "the worst" takes place, it usually makes for a great story.

Regardless, if you stay on the couch, afraid of the worst, you will almost certainly miss out on the best.

Acknowledgements

Book writing is a lot like a marathon—both are viewed as solo endeavors but getting to the finish line of either requires an entire support team. I have a pretty good one.

My parents, Paul and Kathy Moritz, have always nurtured my quirkiness, my dreams, my writing and my athletic goals. To try and thank them adequately is an impossible task.

My brother, Brian Moritz, has been a pain in my side for years. And I love him for it.

My sister-in-law, Jennifer Moritz, has created a cover that inspired and pulled me through on the tough writing days.

My niece, Ellie Moritz, is a spitfire. Watch out for her.

My friend, Alexis Brudnicki, read my early drafts, gave me suggestions, encouraged me and helped me tell my story. We first met in a baseball press box and quickly became running buddies. She inspires me every day.

Scott Kurzdorfer, who told me, matter-of-factly, when something is important to me to "be fierce." I strive to do that every day.

Thank you to Heather Prusak, Nate Lull, Layne Adams, and Carolyn Dragon for early reads, insight and most importantly encouragement. Never underestimate having people in your circle who are excited for dreams because they love you.

About the Author

Amy Moritz is a native of Lockport, New York. She earned a bachelor's degree in journalism/mass communication from St. Bonaventure University and a master's degree in humanities from the University at Buffalo. A sportswriter, she has covered the NFL, NHL, NCAA, and minor league baseball. An endurance athlete and avid hiker, she's probably out running right now. You can find her at www.amymoritz.com. *I Thought You'd Be Faster* is her first book.

84122061R00082

Made in the USA
San Bernardino, CA
03 August 2018